FEATURES

SPRING 2026 • NUMBER 47

Plough

INSIGHTS

DEPARTMENTS

WEB EXCLUSIVES

Read these articles at *plough.com/web47*.

Plough
ANOTHER LIFE IS POSSIBLE

Plough Quarterly No. 47: After Religion
Published by Plough Publishing House, ISBN 978-1-63608-186-1

EDITORIAL OFFICE
151 Bowne Drive
Walden, NY 12586
T: 845.572.3455
info@plough.com

SUBSCRIBER SERVICES
PO Box 8542
Big Sandy, TX 75755
T: 800.521.8011
subscriptions@plough.com

United Kingdom
Brightling Road
Robertsbridge
TN32 5DR
T: +44(0)1580.883.344

Australia
4188 Gwydir Highway
Elsmore, NSW
2360 Australia
T: +61(0)2.6723.2213

Plough Quarterly (ISSN 2372-2584) is published quarterly by Plough Publishing House, PO Box 398, Walden, NY 12586.
Individual subscription $36 / £24 / €28 per year.
Subscribers outside of the United States and Canada pay in British pounds or euros.
Periodicals postage paid at Walden, NY 12586 and at additional mailing offices.
POSTMASTER: Send address changes to Plough Quarterly, PO Box 8542, Big Sandy, TX 75755.

Front cover: Sylwia Perczak, *Lord, Save Me*, acrylic on plywood, 2019. Used by permission.
Inside front cover: Dean L. Mitchell, *St. Augustine Light*, watercolor, 2021. Used by permission.
Back cover: Dean L. Mitchell, *On the Gulf*, watercolor, 2017. Used by permission.

ABOUT THE COVER

Religion can only get you so far; faith alone will save you, as illustrated by the story of Peter walking on the water to Jesus, sinking, and calling out to be saved. This artwork is titled *Lord, Save Me*, by Polish artist Sylwia Perczak.

LETTERS

READERS RESPOND

Readers respond to *Plough*'s Winter 2026 issue, *The Call of Beauty.* Send letters to *letters@plough.com.*

There are at least a couple of articles in each issue that annoy me. But each of the annoying articles is one that I carefully consider and pray about: Why does it rub me the wrong way? How does it challenge my beliefs or values? Is it biblical or is the Bible being misconstrued? The articles achieve your goal of encouraging critical thinking; I encourage you not to jump into the fray of controversial topics for the sake of staying "relevant" or gaining followers who simply want to argue. There is enough of that online. I subscribed to the quarterly because of the gentle way you approach topics, and the peaceful way in which I can consider and meditate on each article. I truly believe many Christians are ready to consider the way of Jesus as loving, kind, and challenging. The way is narrow, but those of us walking along it should be arm in arm in love.

Erika Browning, Duncanville, Texas

On Peter Mommsen's "Dogs, Deer, Herons, and the Promise of Beauty": Peter Mommsen's essay on beauty keeps tightening the circle around the human observer. What troubles me is how narrowly he casts the question of beauty – forever circling back to the human gaze, as though beauty itself waits to be blessed by our perception. To say that creation's loveliness "means" something only insofar as it points to a divine artisan is to mistake beauty for a message. The maple woods, the heron, the deer – all go on being what they are, serenely indifferent to our categories of order or worship.

Beauty does not ask to be moralized or redeemed. It is not a signpost to the Creator, nor a mirror of human virtue or depravity – it precedes all that. The lichen on a boulder, the rot that feeds the forest floor, the glacier's collapse into meltwater – each is beautiful because it simply *is*. To imagine beauty as something that "summons" us is to subtract from its independence. The sacred is not granted by belief; it inheres in existence itself, in the unobserved gleam of things.

The forest does not become less beautiful when no one is there to pray in it; a parasite has its own elaborate form regardless of whether a theologian finds it edifying. To insist that beauty "must *mean* something" is to flatten the world into a set of symbols curated for a single species' spiritual anxieties. The radiance of existence is older and less sentimental than that.

Frederic Page, Desert Hot Springs, California

I consider *Plough* one of my three favorite Christian magazines, and I regularly recommend it to others. My critique comes from someone who is a supporter, an ecumenical Christian, who strives to love everyone without distinction.

I was enjoying your article until I reached the mention of Erika Kirk. I felt that the inclusion of such a controversial figure was distracting – at least it was for me.

I fully accept that truth is truth regardless of its source. However, given the deep concerns many Christians have about the theology promoted by Charlie Kirk and represented and embraced by his wife, I believe quoting her may distract readers from an otherwise excellent article.

Rev. Carlos L. Malave, Concord, Virginia

On Ben Quash's "Layers of Beauty": I really appreciated this interview. Quash noted that the Old Testament contains passages which are aware that "the beauty of appearances can also be a perilous thing," citing Absalom's fatally long hair. A close inspection of 1 and 2 Samuel shows that all references to a person being beautiful in the David story are accompanied by the death of someone related to, or interacting with, the handsome person: David and Goliath, Abigail and Nabal, Bathsheba and Uriah (and her baby with handsome David). The big clue to the danger of relying on appearances appears in 1 Samuel 16:7, when Samuel is scolded for initially selecting one of David's brothers based on appearance: "The Lord doesn't see things the way you see them. People judge by outward appearance, but the Lord looks at the heart."

David Howle, Temple, Texas

On Brandon Vaidyanathan's "My Mother's Hidden Radiance": "Presentability became the conditional price of love." How true this statement often is! We do not fully engage with members of our families and society because they do not look or act like we think they should. I am reminded of the song by Dottie Rambo: "He looked beyond my fault and saw my need." I pray that we will do as Christ does – look beyond fault, sickness, and behavior, and see people's needs.

Linda White,
Newfoundland & Labrador, Canada

On Paul Kingsnorth's "Six Ways to Resist the Machine": This is a bold vision that resonates deeply with me. However, I have one worry. Mr. Kingsnorth's writing on the Machine as it stands here shares, with much anti-modernist writing, the hint of Pelagianism. We have created this mess, it suggests, and we now must get ourselves out of it by our own askesis, or self-discipline. I do not think Kingsnorth is a Pelagian. But to resist this ancient problem, we need something more than discipline and protest. We need grace.

Layton Friesen, Manitoba, Canada

On Natalie Carnes's "Icon or Idol?": Thank you for this thoughtful look at icons and idols; it brings out a theme I have noticed in myself and others. Those who grew up in one faith tradition may find meaning in another – I grew up in a church with no images but have discovered the beauty and meaning that can be found in them without being drawn to worship the images themselves. I've known others who moved in the other direction. I still regularly attend a church without images but often spend time in other places (for services or retreats) that include them.

Katie Oakey, Sydney, Australia

On Charles E. Moore and Stanley Hauerwas's "We Are the Alternative to War": Hauerwas says that, as a Christian, he is committed to nonviolence and that he does not "have a foreign policy because [he's] not a state." I agree that Christians "cannot kill" and that certainly following Jesus' way of nonviolent love is more important for Christians than to follow the demands of any state's foreign policy. However, could not Christians support a world policy if it aimed to do justice and love mercy? Indeed, if such a policy could be formulated – I believe it can – could not Christians endorse measures for doing justice and loving kindness as a way of walking humbly with God? Couldn't they support a nonkilling world policy without diluting their commitment to nonviolence?

Robert Johansen, Oak Park, Illinois

About Us

Plough is published by the Bruderhof, an international community of families and singles seeking to follow Jesus together. Members of the Bruderhof are committed to a way of radical discipleship in the spirit of the Sermon on the Mount. Inspired by the first church in Jerusalem (Acts 2 and 4), they renounce private property and share everything in common in a life of nonviolence, justice, and service to neighbors near and far. There are twenty-nine Bruderhof settlements in both rural and urban locations in the United States, England, Germany, Australia, Paraguay, South Korea, and Austria, with around 3,000 people in all. To learn more or arrange a visit, see the community's website at *bruderhof.com.*

Plough features original stories, ideas, and culture to inspire faith and action. Starting from the conviction that the teachings and example of Jesus can transform and renew our world, we aim to apply them to all aspects of life, seeking common ground with all people of goodwill regardless of creed. The goal of *Plough* is to build a living network of readers, contributors, and practitioners so that, as we read in Hebrews, we may "spur one another on toward love and good deeds."

Plough includes contributions that we believe are worthy of our readers' consideration, whether or not we fully agree with them. Views expressed by contributors are their own and do not necessarily reflect the editorial position of *Plough* or of the Bruderhof communities.

FAMILY & FRIENDS

AROUND THE WORLD

Find Your People

Plough *readers meet in real life.*

Alan Koppschall

In 1920, *Plough*'s founding editor, Eberhard Arnold, wrote that its mission would be to "summon" its readers to "living renewal." His words still serve as *Plough*'s mission statement: "We must get down to the deepest roots of Christianity and demonstrate that they are crucial to solving the urgent problems in contemporary culture. With breadth of vision and energetic daring, our publishing house must steer its course right into the torrent of contemporary thought."

A magazine is more than text and images between two covers or on a screen. The heart of any magazine is the unique assemblage of writers and readers that contribute to it, read it, discuss it, and let it change them. For us, fostering the growth of a community around the magazine means connecting those readers and writers – in real life.

Over the past two years, thousands of *Plough* readers and writers have come together in cities across the United States and United Kingdom for an evening meetup. In 2025, local *Plough* enthusiasts hosted at least twenty-four such events, from Portland to London. At these meetups, readers gather in a café, pub, or private home to connect with other readers from their area and a representative of *Plough* to discuss the latest issue of the magazine and suggest topics they would like to see covered or writers they would like to see published. At least one *Plough* issue, *Freedom*, was a direct result of discussions at a meetup. As one attendee wrote:

> I was struck by how well the meetup created a space for people to share. I was also really fascinated to see so many men in their mid-twenties so earnestly looking for answers to big questions. It was beautiful to see.
>
> I'm very concerned these days by young people who seem to be in danger of going from fear of all commitment to believing that freedom itself is a bad thing and that they need religion because it's a traditional form of limits – not because they see that Jesus is alive and that there is true freedom to be had in the cross. I don't want to be turning anyone away for whatever reason they come to Jesus, but I do worry that we could have a supposedly Christian renaissance that is actually entirely

Alan Koppschall is a Plough *editor and event coordinator. He is a member of the Bruderhof and lives with his wife, Marilyn, in Rifton, New York.*

A *Plough* meetup in London, England.

devoid of Christ. So, it was good to see *Plough* be a really safe and Christ-centered place for people to work out those questions.

My wife and I attended two meetups last year. In Chicago, the group included an old Catholic communitarian, a former Planned Parenthood employee who is now pro-life, and a woman who ran a regenerative farm in Uruguay for eight years with her husband and young family. A couple walked into the café and asked if they could join because it looked interesting. They left as *Plough* readers. Attendees who had never met each other exchanged details and promised to stay in touch.

The Milwaukee meetup was at Panther Catholic, a Newman Center near the city's University of Wisconsin campus. We discussed prayer, health, work, and much more. Several members of a small Catholic intentional community attended. Another attendee has been Wisconsin's official "circus priest" for over a decade, administering the sacrament to Catholics in traveling circus troupes that come through the state. "Sometimes you can find your vocation in the strangest ways," he told us.

At neither meetup were people discussing their political allegiances or grievances. They came looking for something more ordinary but far more powerful: a community of people from the same city who are asking the same questions and looking for a life that in some small way reflects God's kingdom. The renewal that Arnold wrote of in 1920 can begin on the page, but it finds full expression in people gathered around a table and a shared vision. "Where two or three are gathered in my name," Christ says, "there am I among them" (Matt. 18:20).

If you are interested in attending a *Plough* reader meetup, visit *plough.com/events*. If you would like to host a meetup, email *events@plough.com*.

Poet in This Issue

Benjamin P. Myers teaches literature at Oklahoma Baptist University, where he directs the Great Books Honors Program. He was the 2015–16 Poet Laureate of the State of Oklahoma. He is the author of four volumes of poetry – *Elegy for Trains* (2010), *Lapse Americana* (2013), *Black Sunday* (2019), and *The Family Book of Martyrs* (2022) – and several works of nonfiction: *A Poetics of Orthodoxy* (2020), *Ambiguity and Belonging* (2024), and *An Invitation to the Liberal Arts* (2025). Two of his poems in this issue, "A Tang Dynasty Ceramic Horse" (page 11) and "Pear Trees in Winter" (page 41), were selected as finalists (in blind judging) in *Plough's* 2025 Rhina Espaillat Poetry Award. The 2026 contest closes April 30; see past winners and submit your poems at *plough.com/poetryaward.*

SUSTAINING REVIVAL

A Summer Campout Conference

July 31–August 2, 2026

Hosted by *Plough* at the Bruderhof's Fox Hill community in Walden, New York, young adults are welcome to apply for a weekend conference to discuss how to continue to grow in faith and live it out in everyday life. The weekend will consist of conversations, keynotes, and informal discussion, and is free of charge for accepted applicants. Application to attend is open to all between eighteen and thirty.

Learn more at *plough.com/revival.*

Artwork by Anna Dillon. Used by permission.

What Comes After Religion?

The project to forge a Christian society is in retreat. What comes next?

PETER MOMMSEN

JUST SIX YEARS after Constantine the Great bowed his knee to the God of the Christians, he enlisted the church's leadership to serve the Roman empire. In AD 318, bishops were still reeling from the vicious Diocletian persecution, with fresh memories of the torture and execution of their fellow believers. Under a new law, they now gained the power to rule on legal disputes, with their judgments backed by imperial authority and unappealable to civil tribunals. It was a breathtaking reversal of fortune.

Initially, this new judicial role for bishops – the *audientia episcopalis* – amounted to little more than legally binding arbitration: a voluntary alternative to the empire's overburdened and corrupt courts. (Later it would evolve into a fully developed ecclesiastical legal system.) Even at the time, though, Constantine's law marked a first step in the Christianization of state and society, a development that would have far-reaching consequences.

The process of Christianization that Constantine's law inaugurated wasn't a wholesale

Anna Dillon, *The Avenue at Avebury*, oil on board, 1996.

theocratic revolution such as in Iran in 1979. Rather, it advanced fitfully and inconsistently over generations. Beliefs rooted in the New Testament – the sanctity of human life, the rights of the poor, monogamy, the equality of each human being before God – slowly reshaped law and custom. For example, in the two centuries after Constantine, his successors gradually restricted infanticide, gladiatorial games, abortion, forced prostitution, and sexual abduction. They limited the tyranny of creditors over debtors, eased the process for manumission (without abolishing slavery itself), and established organized charity for the poor and a right to asylum in churches. Eventually, Christian legislators introduced the novel idea of consent by both parties in marriage.

Changes in law reflected and spurred on changes in culture. As Christianity spread, the gospel of a crucified God effected a slow-moving yet utterly radical transformation in worldview: Jesus promised that the meek, not the mighty, were the blessed who would inherit the earth. From this transformation, the historian Tom Holland argues in his 2019 book *Dominion*, would eventually spring the modern ideals of emancipation, human rights, and democracy. As a result of the process Constantine began, according to Holland, today Christianity remains – admittedly in a somewhat disguised form – the operating system of the West.

For how long? Today, the process of Christianization launched by Constantine has gone into reverse, at least in the West. According to social scientists, secularization continues apace, as each new generation reports lower rates of belief, religious affiliation, and church attendance than the last. By some accounts, in the United States secularizing trends seem to have slowed in recent years, and some Catholic, Orthodox, and Pentecostal churches in North America and Europe even report upticks in adult baptisms and Sunday attendance, especially by young men. Awakenings on US college campuses have undoubtedly changed individual lives (see page 27).

Yet as the demographer Ryan Burge reports in his new book *The Vanishing Church*, statistically these conversions, however heartening, don't balance out the overall slide in religious belief and practice. As older, more religious cohorts are replaced by younger, less religious ones, Christians appear set to become a minority in the United States just as they have in other countries historically identified with Christendom.

As Christianity has declined demographically over the past fifty years in Western countries, its influence in state and society has declined as well. The spread of support for euthanasia and easy abortion access testifies to the loss of an earlier Christian consensus on the sanctity of human life. Declining marriage rates and the legalization of same-sex unions reflect the collapse of traditional Christian norms in the wake of the sexual revolution. Even falling fertility rates – to below-replacement levels in much of Europe – appear to correlate with growing secularization.

The clearest symptom of de-Christianization, however, has less to do with any given ethical issue than with something more fundamental. Christianity teaches that each human being is made in the image of God, and that humankind, in all its diversity, is one whole. The theological doctrine of equality before God, as Holland reminds us, undergirds any modern appeals to equality under the laws or to intrinsic human rights. And the biblical insistence on the unity of the human race relativizes all divisions between ethnic and national groups. Taken together, these insights are the essential underpinning for liberal democracy.

As Christianity recedes, this legacy is giving way to an age of nihilism – that, at least, is the thesis of the sociologist James Davison Hunter's 2024 book *Democracy and Solidarity*. According to his diagnosis, the vacuum left by de-Christianization is being filled with the naked will to power, whether left- or right-coded. In contrast to Nietzsche's version of the will to power, which claimed to be life-affirming, today's nihilism is marked by what Nietzsche called *ressentiment*, as mutually hostile groups – Hunter terms them "counter-publics" – define themselves against one another by means of "shared narratives of injury." The logic of *ressentiment* pushes people to reject the common search for truth in favor of seeking to crush their group's adversaries. Ultimately such nihilism is incompatible with commitment to universal human dignity and rights. (While Hunter's book focuses specifically on the American experiment, parallels in other Western societies seem clear enough.)

Today, as always, our vocation remains the same: to live already now as citizens of the New Jerusalem.

How are Christians to respond to de-Christianization and its aftereffects? One path is to embrace *ressentiment* and wield Christian identity as a weapon in the nihilistic war of one group against another, at the risk of betraying the very faith one seeks to defend. Prominent figures today have chosen this approach, brandishing Christian words and images in service of anti-Christian ends (see page 42). Alternatively, Christians might abandon the public sphere and retrench, forming cloistered communities to wait out the "new barbarism," to borrow a phrase from Rod Dreher's 2017 book, *The Benedict Option*.

Christians at the time of Constantine's conversion faced similar challenges but adopted a different approach. Their ranks were tiny compared even to the secularized present – they made up perhaps 10 percent of the Roman Empire's population. Like Christians today, they were often internally divided and imperfectly faithful. But despite their demographic insignificance, they possessed a remarkable confidence. As Cardinal Joseph Ratzinger put it (borrowing a phase from Arnold Toynbee), they were a "creative minority," whose power lay not in numbers but in their spiritual vitality and transformed lives. To quote the third-century bishop Cyprian of Carthage, "We are philosophers not in words, but in deeds. . . . We do not speak great things, we live them."

These early believers, understandably grateful as they were that Constantine had embraced the faith and ended persecution, could not have foreseen the centuries-long project of Christianization he would begin: its successes, its abject failures, or what now appears to be its dismantling. Their confidence didn't depend on their group's ability to reform the empire's laws (though they welcomed legislation that reflected the truths of the gospel) or revolutionize their society's mores (though their example eventually had that effect, even if unevenly). Rather, they were certain of Jesus' promise that "the gates of hell will not prevail" against his church in the long run, because he was the Lord of history and would one day return to make all things new.

Christians today, if demoralized, can take courage from these forerunners in the faith. Church decline and the de-Christianization of culture and social institutions are painful and, from a Christian perspective, plainly bad for human beings. But, according to our faith, they aren't the end of the story. Today, as always, our vocation remains the same: to live already now as citizens of the New Jerusalem.

The Nicene Creed reminds us where the future is headed: "He shall come again in glory . . . whose kingdom shall have no end." What will come after Christianity? Christ himself. In the interim, he has given his followers, whether few or many, great things to live and work to do.

A Tang Dynasty Ceramic Horse

It stands on all four hooves, just stopped
as if before a cliffside topped
with waving grasses like its mane.
Ten thousand horses made the plain
resound in one bass voice, as long
as Empress Wu controlled the Tang.
But now in cubed museum glass
just one horse flats the waving grass.
With all that muscle, flesh, and hair
long moldered in the earth's thick care,
this one unbroken horse stands posed,
its eyelids heavy, almost closed.

BENJAMIN P. MYERS

It's Not All Good, Man

How should Christians respond to a church in decline?

KAREN KILBY

DECLINE. SHRINKAGE. BECOMING LESS. Becoming smaller. It's not fun stuff. It doesn't lift the spirits to say these words, or to read them. And yet this has been the experience of many Christian denominations in Europe and North America over half a century and more.

How ought a theologian respond to this situation? Across the course of my career, I've seen two broad strategies from fellow theologians in response to church decline. Both seem to me to be, ultimately, forms of denial.

One approach is to provide a theological diagnosis of what has gone wrong, and then suggest a cure. This approach tries to identify the moment that the key intellectual mistake entered in, perhaps at the beginning of the nineteenth century in the thought of Friedrich Schleiermacher, the "Father of Protestant liberalism." Some go further back, to the seventeenth and eighteenth century Enlightenment, or earlier still, all the way back to the late Middle Ages and the thought of the Franciscan friar Duns Scotus. Or, on the other hand, it is possible to reason in exactly the reverse direction: maybe the problem lies in church and theology not having kept up sufficiently with intellectual and cultural changes around us, being too tradition-bound, too stuck in the mud. Whichever the diagnosis, the cure then follows. If the error came in with Schleiermacher in the nineteenth century or Kant in the eighteenth or Scotus in the fourteenth, the solution will be some kind of retrieval and re-proclamation of a pattern of thought that came before. If the error lay in a failure to keep up with the modern world, the cure must surely lie in reshaping the Christian message as an answer to the deepest questions of contemporary culture.

Many of these diagnoses of our problems are fascinating, and they surely have something to contribute. But to think that they point to *the* answer – that if only we could get our theology right, church decline would be reversed and everything would be wonderful – I have come to believe is a delusion. Theology matters, I am convinced, but I don't think we theologians are

---

Karen Kilby is the Bede Professor of Catholic Theology at Durham University, England.

Abandoned chapel, Occitanie, France, 2018.
Photograph by Romain Veillon.

quite so powerful, quite so much at the center of things, that everything depends on where we go right or wrong.

A second broad strategy seeks not diagnosis and cure, but re-evaluation. In my more irreverent moments, inspired by the well-known Bob Odenkirk character, I think of this as the Saul Goodman strategy. As some readers will know, the central character from the *Better Call Saul* television series derives his name from his own earlier catch phrase, "It's all good, man." According to this second theological response, what first appears to be loss is not truly loss at all, but gain. Numbers declining, buildings sold off, Christian belief on the wane? It might seem a bit grim, but if only you know how to look at it, really, it's all good, man.

Often this is articulated in terms of an escape from Constantinianism. Constantine the Great, the Roman emperor from 306 to 337, converted to Christianity sometime around 312 or 313, and not only legalized the Christian faith but also offered various financial and political advantages to the church. In Eusebius's classic account of Constantine's conversion, the emperor had a vision of a cross on the eve of an important (and ultimately successful) battle, together with the phrase "by this sign you shall conquer": so the cross becomes associated with military might, and the church entangled with imperial power.

Quite a range of theologians argue that what we experience in secularization and church decline is the end of Constantinianism, and therefore to be welcomed: a liberation from political capture. The church is losing what it never should have had: the patronage of power, entanglement with the state, the benefits of establishment. These were corrupting influences. In being stripped of them, the church can be more truly itself, more faithful to Christ. So, indeed, it's all good, man: apparent loss is, in truth, gain.

Might the recent rise in Christian nationalism call into question the idea that we are moving beyond the Constantinian era of the church's life? Perhaps. But in any case, there is another difficulty with this story. What is lost, as church membership and church practice diminish, is not just the bad bits. It may be that there is some useful purgation when the churches lose their default position in society, their association with the status quo, their inside track to power. But there are many other things that disappear as churches decline, things that were valuable and precious.

Let me give a couple of examples. The vagaries of my career as a lay Catholic theologian have led to time spent in recent years with women religious, contemplative nuns and sisters engaged in active ministry, teaching, chaplaincy, spiritual direction, and so on. In particular, through a research project, I enjoyed a close engagement with the Congregation of La Retraite, a religious community with its origins in seventeenth-century Brittany, which is now facing the possibility of its own end. It has been an enriching set of encounters, probably the only part of my working life where I have felt genuinely outside the corporately organized, neoliberal world. The sisters I have met are good listeners, often with a certain quality of presence, often striking me as holy people. Overall, my sense is that they are countercultural in a quiet but very powerful way.

Many such congregations are having to reckon with their own dwindling, and sometimes their approaching end. There is something moving about the calm, clear-eyed, unresentful way the sisters I know navigate this. For the most part, they do so without recrimination or complaint, but also without denying the difficulty and pain that is part of the process. And yet I have the sense that the loss of their communities will be a true loss for both church and society. There is a collective way of being in the world and in the church that is distinctive and valuable, and that simply won't be available to us – in this particular way, in any case – in the future.

Abandoned chapel, Brittany, France, 2021.
Photograph by Romain Veillon.

Or think about a parish that ceases to exist. At the time of its closing, perhaps the congregation is very small, very elderly; perhaps if they were to try to cling on, it might be seen as unrealistic, sentimental, nostalgic. But the loss is real. It is real for those who may have lifelong connections to the particular place and the dynamism it once

represented, perhaps even memories of their parents raising the funds to build the church. But there is another loss, even if it is never noticed. It is about what will not be there for those who come later, or rather for those who don't – those who might have had something deep and valuable, a living faith, sparked from what they might have encountered if that parish church had continued as living reality. Of course, in times past, some or many who went to church did so out of convention and habit only. But it is not only the ones who might have developed into merely nominal, merely social, Christians who won't in the future encounter the church. There are also those for whom faith might have become something real, for whom it would have reshaped their inner landscapes, the way they see the world, their life's course, who will now perhaps never truly encounter the gospel because of the closing of this and other parishes. One does not have to be preoccupied with hell, anxious over questions of eternal salvation or damnation, to understand such an absence as genuine loss.

Sometimes church diminishment is cast in terms of kenosis, "self-emptying." The famous hymn Paul quotes in his letter to the Philippians speaks of Christ, who "did not regard equality with God as something to be exploited, but emptied himself, taking on the form of a slave" (Phil. 2:6–7). If self-emptying was the movement Christ made in the Incarnation, surely it must be a good thing for the church as well. I regularly see theologians commending a kenotic church and encouraging us to think of the diminishment we experience in these terms.

For a couple of reasons I find myself suspicious of calls for ecclesial kenosis. True enough, there are forms of wealth and influence the church has had that it never should have. Perhaps it is a good thing when these wither away. But ought we really speak of this loss of outsized privilege and power by analogy with the perfect generosity of the eternal Son of God's Incarnation? Surely this is a subtle reinforcement of the very arrogance we need to leave behind, a way to cling on, even as we grow weaker, to our grandiosity.

When what is at issue is the loss of power and prestige that never should have been the church's, the language we need to reach for describes ecclesial purgation, perhaps something like collective repentance or *metanoia*. On the other hand, when the issue is different, a change that means the church is less able to give witness to the gospel in a particular place or in a particular way, why dress this real loss up in positive clothing, why cast it as imitation of Christ's Incarnation?

But if we are to reject the Saul Goodman approach – if things are *not* "all good, man" – what then? Can believing that everything is *not* in fact all good be compatible with trust in Providence and in the Holy Spirit's guidance of the church? Indeed, if I am suggesting that we should neither put our trust in diagnosis and cure for ecclesial

Abandoned church, Donegal, Ireland, 2016. Photograph by Romain Veillon.

decline, nor try to redescribe our situation so that we can be easily reconciled with it, what will I propose instead?

My hunch is that there is some light to be shed on church decline if we think of it as a form of suffering. For some, at least, this must surely be what it is. The church's shrinking will not be, for most of us, the most acute form of suffering imaginable, the most dramatic or the deepest. But to watch the decay of what one worked to build; to have a sense that things which are close to one's heart, which most illumine and motivate, matter less and less to others; to see that there has been a failure of transmission, of witness, down the generations, that the institution is getting older, weaker, less relevant, less respected; to see less and less external validation of what seems to one most meaningful – all these things come together to impose a sort of collective suffering, at least to those who remain in churches in the West.

For some years I have been exploring the place of suffering in Christian thought, and I have come to think that we stand between two temptations: a flight from suffering, and an embrace of it. The flight is perhaps the simpler thing to recognize: as a culture we are inclined to associate suffering with failure, to assume that if we make enough scientific, technical, and economic progress, and if we conduct our affairs with sufficient optimism, it is ultimately possible to avoid all suffering. One will be able to be happy and fulfilled, as well as productive, if only one maintains the right attitude, reads the right self-help books, and establishes a good morning routine.

The embrace of suffering is less obvious, but it seems to me also a temptation, particularly within the church. We know that there is something amiss with the secular culture's flight from suffering, and we have the cross as our central paradigm, where love and suffering both reach a high point. So there can be a temptation to sacralize suffering, to fuse love and suffering, or holiness and suffering, to see suffering as itself the path that leads to God. There's a subtle difference, but an important one, between enduring the suffering that is sometimes necessary *on* the path to God, and embracing suffering *as* the path to God.

Yet there is, I think, an alignment between the strategies with which I began and these two temptations. The "diagnose and cure" response to church decline can be a form of flight from suffering. It is difficult to contemplate the fact that the project in which you are involved, the church you love, is on the wane, that the enormously rich, long, fascinating spiritual and intellectual tradition in which you are immersed is increasingly marginal and irrelevant. Perhaps the hunt for the theological moment where it all went wrong, and the theological pivot which will make it all OK, is a way of looking away, of suppressing the pain, of not facing the grimness and difficulty of the moment.

Can believing that everything is *not* in fact all good be compatible with trust in Providence and in the Holy Spirit's guidance of the church?

But the Saul Goodman approach, the Constantinian and kenotic themes, are aligned with a potentially dangerous temptation to embrace suffering. The smaller the church gets, the more irrelevant it seems, the more we can rejoice, because the more secretly holy it will turn out to be. If we look through sufficiently spiritual eyes, we will see that loss can be embraced as gain – it's all good, man.

How else might we go about thinking about decline in our churches? I'd like to propose that reflection on death as we meet it in the lives of ordinary individuals might prove helpful. What is at stake in ecclesial decline is not the death of

Abandoned Catholic college, Nouvelle Aquitaine, France, 2015.
Photograph by Romain Veillon.

the church of Christ as such, but there can be an ending for particular communities, particular movements, particular cultures.

When a person dies, sometimes it is his own "fault" – he didn't exercise enough, she didn't watch her cholesterol, he didn't look before he crossed the street. But we all know that death, even early death, is not always the fault of the one who dies. People may die after bringing to a graceful conclusion all their major life projects and longings, fulfilling all the potential that was in them. But we all know that death does not always wait for that moment: often enough, death interrupts a life not yet lived fully, projects that were not completed, potentials that could never be realized.

When some expression of the church – a parish, a youth movement, a tradition of preaching, a religious order – comes to an end, we can say something similar. It might be that someone in leadership has failed to read the world around them well enough, has failed in some other way in handing down a distinctive tradition or vision. But maybe not. It may be no one's fault, simply a matter of social forces larger than us all. And again, sometimes it may be that an institution, a movement, a religious order, comes to an end at a time when its particular gifts are no longer needed, when they have completed their work. But maybe not. In our current fragmented times, we have more need than ever for the distinctive witness, presence, and attentiveness I have met among Catholic religious sisters. Nevertheless, many of these groups will disappear, at least from Europe and North America.

So I am persuaded that sadness and mourning, together with a bit of gratitude for what once existed, in all its beauty, is sometimes the right response to decline and diminishment. We don't always need to assign blame or feel responsible for finding a solution.

Alongside the sadness and mourning, there must always be a recognition that loss is not the whole of the story. In some parts of the world, the church is in growth, not decline. Even where it is not growing, new things emerge, new movements, new possibilities, new ways of giving witness. And surely we trust that the grace of God is at work in ways we do not know and cannot imagine outside the boundaries of what we recognize as "church."

It's not an either-or. Sadness about what is lost, and recognition of new growth and new possibility are not at odds with one another: we can think and feel two things at once, and one doesn't cancel the other out in some tidy mathematical equation.

While I am not much of a fan of the Saul Goodman approach, I do feel an attachment to Julian's. Julian of Norwich famously insists that "all shall be well, and all shall be well, and all manner of thing shall be well." What's the difference? Aren't they just alternate slogans for the same overarching optimism? The difference is in the tense of the verb. Julian is not asking us to think that all is now well, that all manner of things are already as they ought to be in the world we see around us, or in the church we see around us. She is instead transmitting a trust that, beyond anything we can understand or plan for, all *shall* be well. Her theological vision is deep, beautiful, hopeful, and full of trust, but as I read her, at least, in what it purports to understand, to integrate, and to explain, it is remarkably restrained.

I think this is a proper Christian disposition. It's not all good, man. It's sad, dispiriting, and depressing at times to see diminishment in the churches around us. But sadness and bleakness can never be the whole story. We do what we have it in us to do, we appreciate and rejoice in the elements of new growth and possibility we can detect even in the midst of diminishment, and finally, we trust that the Holy Spirit will not abandon the church. We know that its ultimate future, together with the future of all things and all manner of things, does not depend on our own best analyses and strategies.

The Gods of Modernity

Today's world is not disenchanted. It is furiously enchanted.

GALEN WATTS

Anne Desmet, *Babel/Vesuvius,* linocut, wood engraving, print, and collage on paper, 2002.

In 1917, the German sociologist Max Weber delivered a stirring speech at the University of Munich to a hall full of students and faculty. The topic of his address was what it takes to make it in the profession of science; Weber was a stern man and a proud scientist, who believed that only those single-mindedly devoted to the scientific ideal should pursue it. But Weber's lecture, "Science as a Vocation," is rarely remembered for its career counseling; rather, what has endured is the account of modern life that framed his advice. "The fate of our times," Weber famously declared, "is characterized by rationalization and intellectualization and, above all, by the 'disenchantment of the world.'"

Weber's impassioned remarks about "disenchantment" have become lodestones of sociological lore. But their influence extends far beyond it, animating a broad common feeling about the world. That the modern world is "disenchanted" has become something of a cliché. Yet like most clichés, the truth it points to has been buried beneath layers of misunderstanding.

Weber is known for articulating a *tragic* account of modernity – the tragedy resides at the intersection of two facts. The first is the supremacy of science and technology in modern institutions. And the second is the deep human need for transcendent moral meaning.

The modern world is shaped by the forces of science and technology. In every domain of our lives – from what we eat and consume to how we travel and work – we rely upon technological expertise. Ours is a society premised upon the domestication of nature for our own instrumental ends; through science and technology we seek mastery of the world. Because of the immense instrumental power unleashed by science, Weber observed, it takes an outsized role in public arguments about what is true or good. Modernity, he noted, institutionalizes a spirit of rational calculation at the expense of substantive values.

The tragedy of modern disenchantment arises, then, from the fact that, for all its instrumental power, science cannot provide the metaphysical or moral succor humans desperately need. Citing Tolstoy, Weber remarks, "Science is meaningless because it gives no answer to our question, the only question important for us: 'What shall we do and how shall we live?'" Here lies the modern predicament: science and technology have given us unprecedented instrumental power yet excised the sources of moral meaning upon which human flourishing depends.

Science gives us power, but it cannot tell us what to live for.

Secularization Theory and Its Weaknesses

In the field of sociology, secularization theory – the account of religion's decline in the modern world – is profoundly indebted to Weber. In fact, it would not be unfair to say the theory is merely a refinement and expansion of Weber's Munich address. Secularization theorists view the decline of Christianity in the West as chiefly the result of processes of "disenchantment" – that is, the rising authority of science, the replacement of religious ritual by technology, and the codification of instrumental rationality across modern institutions.

Secularization theory sees science and technology as undermining and displacing Christian belief and practice. A premodern Christian farmer, faced with drought, would pray for rain;

Galen Watts is an assistant professor in the Department of Sociology and Legal Studies at the University of Waterloo, Ontario. His book The Spiritual Turn *(Oxford University Press, 2022) examines the shift from "religion" to "spirituality" that has, in recent years, transformed the religious landscape of the West.*

Max Weber, 1918.

now the farmer simply turns on some sprinklers. But I'm skeptical of this account. Belief in ghosts, fairies, and spirits remains widespread in the twenty-first century; ours is far from a rationalist paradise, as Pew surveys make clear. What is more, many Christians – both historically and in the present day – have had little trouble reconciling science and religion. In fact, according to sociologist Elaine Howard Ecklund, professional scientists around the world routinely combine rigorous scientific practice with personal faith. Science properly understood is silent on the question of moral meaning and so cannot tell us what values or projects to commit to. In this sense, science simply *cannot* replace *religion*.

What the Weber story fails to see is that Christianity's decline derives less from the ascendance of science than from the falling out of fashion of what Notre Dame sociologist Christian Smith calls "traditional Christianity."

When Westerners think of "religion," we tend to think about churches, priests, pastors, and the like; that is, we associate "religion" with the types of Christianity that have been historically dominant – think mainline Protestantism in the United States, Anglicanism in Britain, Catholicism in France – traditional Christianity. Beginning in the Enlightenment but culminating in the 1960s, traditional Christianity ("religion") became coded throughout the West as anti-modern, oppressive, and intellectually suspect. For countercultural youth, "religion" represented everything that was wrong with the world. Baby boomers weren't against *religion* or spiritual feeling (as the blossoming of the New Age Movement demonstrates), but rather opposed "religion" (again, traditional Christianity). This explains why the real drop in churchgoing begins not in the nineteenth century with the rise of science, but in the 1960s.

Many moderns reject Christian practices, not because they are irrational, but because they are uncool.

In his recently published *Why Religion Went Obsolete: The Demise of Traditional Faith in America*, Smith bolsters this thesis, while deepening it considerably. He contends that the decline of traditional Christianity in America has very little to do with the spread of science. Instead it has a great deal to do with the consolidation of a resolutely *anti*-Christian culture. On this view, the world we inhabit is less *post-religious* than post-"religious." Many moderns – especially the young – have rejected traditional Christianity as a viable route to salvation. They see Christian values and virtues as antiquated and anathema. They reject Christian beliefs and practices, not because they are irrational, but because they are uncool.

But our religious yearnings are not easily shaken off. Weber believed that the religious impulse stems from the fact that humans require frameworks of meaning to motivate us, guide our behavior, and give purpose to our lives. Without these, we experience nothing short of existential terror. When each of us wakes up in the morning, we face the question: What shall I devote myself to? To answer this question, says Weber, is inherently *religious*, for it presupposes a faith in something that transcends us. Humans require a soteriology – an account of life's ultimate meaning, a commanding moral framework, a promise of salvation. For Weber, owing to the spread of science in modernity, this need is frustrated for most contemporary people. Yet, again, it does not – cannot – disappear. So what becomes of it?

Taking Weber seriously leads one to the conclusion that disenchantment inevitably spurs *re-enchantment*. If humans are made to seek salvation, it is unlikely that we will be able to tolerate a "disenchanted" order for very long. No – we will seek salvation in something because, well, that's just what we do.

This is why secularization theory, for all its insight, is deeply mistaken. The modern world is indeed pervaded by science and technology; rationalization and intellectualization have made inroads into almost every domain of human life – from social policy to our sex lives. Yet, far from being wholly "disenchanted," the twenty-first century is furiously enchanted – plural sources of salvation are multiplying and competing for our souls. Modernity is less a secular wasteland than an arena of warring gods. There are too many to name, but four contenders stand out: the self, work, politics, and technology.

Seeking After Modernity's Gods

The first god of modernity is the self. A legacy of the Romantic movement is its preoccupation with immanence, subjectivity, inner feeling, and expressiveness. Contemporary romantics chase pure experience and personal authenticity. Their soteriological end is self-realization. To become one's "true self" is a principal moral commandment of secular modernity.

The romantic quest for salvation through self-realization is most apparent in the rise of "spiritual but not religious" self-identification. In rejecting "religion," people who claim to be

The romantic quest for salvation through self-realization is most apparent in the rise of the "spiritual but not religious."

spiritual nevertheless aim to reject conformity, dogmatism, and collectivism – which they associate (rightly or wrongly) with traditional Christianity. "Spirituality," on the other hand, is said to be expressive, open-minded, and individual. Not surprisingly, the "spiritual but not religious" cohort has close historical ties to the liberation movements of the 1960s, from feminism to gay liberation. In their own ways, these movements endorsed a shared soteriology of self-realization, laying the groundwork for what philosopher Charles Taylor calls our late modern "culture of authenticity." To question the sacredness of personal authenticity now constitutes heresy.

Of course, Christians do, and should, care about authenticity. What is more, the sacralization of self has been instrumental to the spread of belief in human rights. But the quest for self-realization has evolved in strange, dark directions in recent years.

On the gnostic left, the ideal of self-realization sees all societal traditions and norms as oppressive and tyrannical, as forcing individuals into boxes at odds with their subjective sense of themselves. This is what leads a striking number of youth to oppose not merely restrictive gender norms, but the mundane belief that sex is binary. From the vantage point of untrammeled self-assertion, the categories of male and female can only be

Artwork by Anne Desmet. Used by permission.

experienced as violent impositions. If societal norms conflict with one's inner feelings, then the norms must go.

Ironically – and frighteningly – the Nietzschean devotion to raw self-assertion is now finding traction on the political right. The Left's great mistake was assuming that the sacralization of subjectivity would naturally support progressive ends. Yet, as the popularity of "vitalist" spokespeople like Bronze Age Pervert makes clear, the Left has no monopoly on the soteriology of self-realization. If God and self are one, morality is what you make it. For the radical right, genuine self-realization demands that the strong do what they want, while the weak suffer what they must.

Here we meet another god warring for dominance: work. What gives work its salvific quality stems, in part, from its relationship to wealth. Under modern capitalism, mammon takes on a mystical quality. To be sure, in all ages wealth has been mistaken for a sign of divine blessing. But in highly stratified societies, wealth is both a status symbol and an entry pass to social acceptance. To lack wealth can mean social death. Yet especially for the educated upper-middle classes, work is not valued merely for the prosperity it promises; it's increasingly looked to as a source of transcendent moral meaning. When surveyed in 2018 about what gives their lives meaning, 48 percent of high-income and college-educated Americans reported that it was their jobs.

While seeing one's labor as having spiritual value is by no means foreign to Christianity, it would be wrong to interpret these findings merely as a survival of the Protestant ethic. As the writer Derek Thompson notes, the trend in recent years is not viewing one's career as consonant with one's religious vocation but rather replacing religion with work – what he calls "workism." In a similar vein, the Berkeley sociologist Carolyn Chen argues in *Work Pray Code* that instead of investing their lives in a religious congregation, as was once an American norm, the upper-middle classes increasingly invest themselves in their jobs – to

Anne Desmet, *Babel Tower in Pieces (Homage to Bruegel)*, 1999, wood engraving and linocut on paper.

the great detriment of their families, friendships, neighborhoods, and communities.

For those who doubt that work serves as a source of salvation, recall that for Weber religion concerns the question: What shall I devote myself to? Ours is a world where the professional-managerial classes desperately pursue redemption through productivity, self-optimization, and ever more achievement: one more line on the CV, one more degree, one more title. The promise of salvation is, one prays, just around the corner. Moreover, in the age of AI, the threat of damnation in the form of unemployment becomes all too real. The modern quest for self-optimization is Sisyphean; optimization presupposes an ultimate end. Optimization for what? To make more money, to produce more, to achieve more. But to what end? The god of work looms like a slavedriver, always present but never satisfied.

Another god that vies for our loyalty is politics. One need only recall the utopian movements that tore through the twentieth century, fueled by a this-worldly desire for salvation: communism on the left, fascism on the right. At the heart of the soteriology of politics is a belief that religious redemption can and should be achieved through political struggle.

The term "wokeness" is generally used pejoratively, and many critics have mocked the phenomenon by analogizing it to religion. But the analogy warrants our consideration. The doyen of antiracism, Ibram X. Kendi, confesses in the opening pages of his 2019 bestseller, *How to Be an Antiracist,* that his zeal for social justice stems directly from his upbringing in the Black church, and the soteriological strivings it cultivated in him. Whatever else one might say about this, it exemplifies perfectly the transference of religious yearnings into political ones – a process that has become commonplace on both the left and right.

In the "enchanted" 1600s, Catholics and Protestants waged war to defend their theological commitments. Today, few millennials or Gen Zers even know the difference between Catholicism and Protestantism. Yet ask them if they would be willing to date someone of an opposing political tribe and the knives will come out. It is not questions about the nature of God that foment our contemporary "religious wars," it is questions about gender, race, and immigration.

Today, few millennials or Gen Zers even know the difference between Catholicism and Protestantism. Yet ask them if they would be willing to date someone of an opposing political tribe and the knives will come out.

As politics has risen to become a dominant source of salvation, polarization is the natural outcome. If our soul's redemption depends upon our having the "right" politics, then political disagreement becomes intolerable. Moreover, political messianism raises the stakes of democracy to unbearable heights. Every election becomes a matter of deliverance or damnation.

There is one final modern god competing for our worship: science. Much of "Science as a Vocation" involves Weber cautioning his fellow scientists against looking to science for what it cannot ultimately deliver – moral meaning. In this way, one can find in Weber a powerful critique of Richard Dawkins's paeans to the inherent meaningfulness of science. His faults notwithstanding, Weber was admirably consistent; true courage, he argued, demanded that moderns resist "enchanting" science and technology (what amounts to "scientism").

We have spectacularly failed to heed Weber's counsel. Ours is not merely a "rationalized" society, it's shot through with a techno-utopianism that treats science and technology as the lone routes to personal and collective salvation. This techno-utopianism is most apparent in Silicon Valley, where self-appointed priests of technological progress like Elon Musk and Marc Andreessen employ their inordinate wealth and power to steamroll us into a future of their making. But it equally lives on in the commonsense assumptions that lead so many to confuse the virtual with the real, to fall spellbound before every new gadget, and to treat technological adoption as an iron law of nature. One of the great follies of secularization theory has been its failure to see that science and technology are invested with immense moral and religious significance, that they serve as the mythic anchors of an Enlightenment narrative of perpetual progress, while animating our near-boundless Promethean grandiosity.

The question remains: "What shall we do, and how shall we live?"

The most paradoxical aspect of the modern deification of technology is that, while it begins as a promise of human emancipation – from scarcity, sickness, and mortality – it ends in dehumanization. The motivation for pursuing artificial general intelligence (AGI), our tech overlords readily admit, is to transform humans into gods. What is never mentioned is that achieving this would entail ridding ourselves of everything that makes us truly human, from our frailty and dependence to our capacity to love and die. Thus the god of technology is perhaps the most dangerous of all, for it commands us to betray our very humanity.

These are a few of the gods that war for our souls in this "disenchanted" age. Of course, as has always been the case, these gods can, and do, find common cause, forging alliances here and there. But like all gods, they are jealous and harbor imperial ambitions; they desire our undivided loyalty.

Christians may read this and think: *these are not gods, they are idols.* I would not disagree, but Weber's sociological perspective helps us cast our present condition in a new light and realize how many Christians unknowingly worship at their altars – a fact in no small part responsible for diminishing the moral standing of the church. Either way, when we remove our sociological lenses, we are still faced with, as Weber puts it, "the only question important for us: 'What shall we do and how shall we live?'"

There have been murmurings about a Christian revival, about youth flocking back to the churches. What should we make of these claims? As the religious commentator Ryan Burge notes, the claim that there is a religious revival taking place among the young is an extraordinary one, which requires extraordinary evidence to prove. That incontrovertible evidence does not exist, at least yet. Of course, anything is possible, but I agree with Christian Smith that we inhabit a culture that is inimical and alien to that of traditional Christianity. So, while I can absolutely envisage a religious revival taking place, I am not confident it will be Christian in any recognizable sense.

This is not to say genuine Christian piety is nowhere to be found. It is to suggest that to be a committed Christian in the twenty-first century is to be profoundly *counter*cultural. In the world we inhabit today, to live by the gospel requires principled conviction, concerted discipline, and purposeful community. In a sense, the task is much harder than it once was. And this is indeed a sobering thought. Yet it's worth remembering that Christianity emerged into a world not unlike our own – where jealous gods warred for our attention and loyalty. Thus, in a deeper sense, it is no harder now than it ever was to walk in the footsteps of Jesus.

TIMOTHY J. KEIDERLING

What Set Off the Asbury Outpouring?

The university's president talks about the 2023 revival and its ongoing effects.

If you ask Kevin Brown, president of Kentucky's Asbury University, about what, alongside the Holy Spirit, set the stage for the Asbury Outpouring – the February 2023 chapel service that turned into sixteen days of revival and renewal – he will probably say something about desperation. There were other things that helped, but desperation, more than anything, drove them to that point. At least, that is what he said when I spoke to him recently.

Asbury University has had a long history of revival; there have been nine separate occasions in the school's history when chapel services or prayer groups spilled out into wider movements. For some reason, all of them have happened in February or March. The biggest and most far-reaching ones took place in 1950 and 1970, when as a result of the revivals, "witness teams" spread out across the country to other colleges and universities, and tens of thousands of people reportedly experienced conversion or renewal.

In Brown's view, many in Gen Z are uniquely positioned for renewal because of their distress. He said he noticed a kind of "low wattage nihilism" in most of his Gen Z students. They are "fatigued by the scripts that have been handed to them," and they are ready to act, to do, to get off the sidelines. During and after the Outpouring (a title chosen by Asbury folks to differentiate it from the earlier Asbury revivals), the prayer requests from Asbury undergraduates were desperate: they prayed about depression, anxiety, suicide, and addiction. They were crying out for something new, Brown said. He heard that cry audibly on the last day of the Outpouring. Look at the last few years, he told me. We've seen war, pandemic, unrest, political uncertainty. And by the phones students placed on the altar, he could

---

Timothy J. Keiderling is a member of the Bruderhof. He lives with his wife and three children at Woodcrest, a community in New York.

Photographs courtesy of Asbury University.

tell that technology hasn't helped make things better for them.

What do they want instead? For one thing, they "valorize authenticity." For Gen Z students, Brown said, "the brochure needs to match reality." They want something genuine, something real. It was that hunger that most prepared the campus and its students for the Outpouring. One conversation he had with a student helped him understand the wishes and hopes of many young people. The student told him that they don't want something more – in the sense of more content, more filler, more extras. They want something less. But they want that less to be authentic.

I asked Brown what it was about the Outpouring that had made him realize that they had to just let it happen, that they couldn't stand in the way. I wanted to know why some well-meaning administrator hadn't just encouraged the students to get back to class and get on with their day. I myself attended two private Christian colleges during my undergraduate studies, both of which had mandatory chapel services, so I'm familiar with how, every now and then, a spurt of interest, a sudden hunger for God to work, can arise in students who are reminded of it every week, multiple times per week. What made this time different? It was mostly a matter of imagination and humility, Brown said. Imagination, because at that time, the staff and administration asked, "What if this might be God stirring our students?" What if God really was doing something? What if this time, they should not "be quick to put our thumb on this"?

It was an ordinary chapel service, on an ordinary day, one of three weekly services held on the Asbury campus. Brown was quick to tell me that most students don't like chapel. But while he tries to avoid causal language, the night before the Outpouring, a gospel choir had been praying intensely "over every seat in the chapel." There were little things that prepared the way, and all of them helped.

Humility was the other big part of it, according to Brown. "I was in such awe," he said. In his view, "a spiritual space opens up when we are humble." And all of that – the desperation, the quiet brokenness of the students, and the openness to see whether God really was doing something – cleared the way for the Outpouring to happen.

The way it happened still surprises him. Nineteen or twenty students stayed in the auditorium to pray after 11:00 a.m., when the chapel service ended. But then they didn't leave. When Brown heard about it, he started clearing his schedule, canceling meetings. By evening, hundreds of students had joined those in the auditorium. The next few days, he said, were "lovely." There was testimony; there was confession; there was healing of brokenness, and reports of physical healing too. It all felt entirely authentic, entirely "unedited." It was only after several days that the world arrived, and through those first days, he could tell that everyone in the staff and administration shared his urge to step back, to see what would happen, to allow God to work.

Toward the end of our conversation, I asked Brown what convinced him that what was happening was genuine. He pointed to several things. First, the authenticity and vulnerability of the students; second, what he saw among the staff: self-sacrifice unlike anything he was used to from them, and "godly hospitality." And then, during the course of the Outpouring and afterward, lives were changed, and real, significant commitments made.

I wanted to know if, after several years, the Asbury campus felt different. Did the Outpouring have any lasting effects? He smiled and told me that he wished he could say that most of the student body were wearing monks' robes. They aren't, but he still holds that "something important is stirring," not just at Asbury but around the world. The question, then, is whether we will have the imagination and the humility to let it happen.

KING-HO LEUNG

The Critique of Religion

What if Christianity is not the religion we thought it was?

"THE CRITIQUE OF RELIGION is the prerequisite of all critique."

So wrote Karl Marx in the opening line of his *Critique of Hegel's "Philosophy of Right."* To call into question the existing order of the world, Marx argued, we must call into question those systems of thought which lead us to take that order for granted. As Marx saw it, religion was one such oppressive "ideology": a set of rules, beliefs, and social conventions upholding the institutions and power structures of the status quo. "Religion" – by which Marx primarily means Christianity – seeks to keep the wealthy wealthy and the poor poor: it tells you that your ultimate

---

King-Ho Leung is an assistant professor in Theology, Philosophy and the Arts at King's College London. He is the author of Spiritual Life and Secular Thought: A Phenomenology *(Oxford University Press, 2026).*

Carlijn Kingma, *A History of the Utopian Tradition*, Chinese ink on paper, 2016 (detail).

value is in some place called "heaven," so you don't have to worry about economic inequality or poverty during your time on earth. The Christian Gospels tell us, "blessed are the poor," "blessed are the meek," "blessed are the peacemakers": in other words, Marx opines, the Christian religion teaches that the poor should accept their poverty, the meek should accept their place, and the peacemakers shouldn't put up a fight against injustice. This is why Marx strikingly calls religion "the opium of the people": it soothes the pain you experience in the real world by sending you to sleep. To be free from oppression, in Marx's view, requires that we free ourselves from the illusions keeping us oppressed: that's why "the critique of religion is the prerequisite of all critique."

Marx believed that, as society moved from feudalism toward capitalism, religion would inevitably decline. The nearly two centuries since Marx wrote those memorable lines have undoubtedly witnessed a decline in religious belief and practices. Even though there have been reports of renewed interest in religion among younger generations, twenty-first-century Western society has become less religious by almost any metric. One particularly interesting phenomenon emerging

from this long decline witnessed in recent years is the emerging social demographic of the "spiritual but not religious": people who explicitly identify as not belonging to any "religion," yet who still see themselves as "spiritual."

But what does it mean to be "spiritual but not religious"? Is such "spirituality" really that different from "religion"? Many scholars argue that it's not. In their view, the spirituality of the so-called "spiritual but not religious" is often just an eclectic "pick 'n' mix" of ideas and practices from traditional religions. There are other ways of construing secular or nonreligious spirituality. But in the dominant scholarly view, the "spiritual but not religious" phenomenon is nothing but a kind of individualized, consumerized, even commodified version of traditional religion. In other words, the "spirituality" of the "spiritual but not religious" is a spirituality of capitalism: a peculiar expression of traditional religiosity under the socioeconomic conditions of capitalism, with capitalism replacing religion as late modernity's principal ideology. Some followers of Marx might even say that what we call capitalism is itself *also* a kind of religion, operating according to a crypto-theological structure of belief. It is just that, instead of God, we now believe in money.

Where "God" was once held as the source of all value, the "value of all values" by which we evaluate things, this role is now played by money. We no longer find the value and worth of things in God, but *in money*: a North London house in Highgate (where Marx is buried) is *worth* more, is more *valuable* than an East London flat not because it is holier, but because we are told by money that it has a higher price tag. When we speak of "what I am *worth*" in our everyday speech, we no longer refer to any notion of inherent dignity; rather, "what I am *worth*" now literally refers to the value of possessions I have or how much I have in the bank.

Consequently, if we regard capitalism as a kind of religion, then, counterintuitively, you could say

Details from Carlijn Kingma, *A History of the Utopian Tradition.*

we're now actually more religious than ever in our all-encompassing money-driven world. For while in a pre-capitalist traditional religious society, one may privately hold a rejection of religion and deny the existence of God; one cannot reject money or deny its existence or the power it has over our lives. We all – one way or another, whether we call it "religious" or not – *believe in* money. We not only accept its existence but evaluate the worth of things and people in terms of money. In the old parlance, we no longer put our faith in God, we put it in mammon.

The claim that capitalism is a kind of religion is, of course, not without its problems. Unlike traditional religions, people don't tend to identify themselves as "capitalists" as they might as Buddhists, Christians, or Muslims. We don't (usually) find people going into their banks as a place of worship to profess their belief in money. To claim that capitalism is a religion perhaps raises more problems than it answers: If capitalism is a religion, then aren't many other cultural phenomena also religions? To think of the case at hand, isn't a Marxist outlook on society – as many critics of Marx have suggested – itself a kind of religion? After all, people are more likely to explicitly and proudly identify themselves as Marxists than to profess to be convicted of free-market ideals. Just as certain religious groups may be identified by the way they dress, we are more likely to see people wearing t-shirts with Marx's or Che Guevara's faces on them than Friedrich Hayek's. Like how many religions have their authoritative texts and canonical scriptures – we can probably find more people devoting time to studying the classic texts of Marx, Engels, and the rest of the Marxian tradition than votaries of Adam Smith's *Wealth of Nations* – or even Donald Trump's *The Art of the Deal.*

But even if one admits that Marxism is no less a religious tradition than capitalism, the problem remains: if capitalism is a religion, Marxism is a religion, football is a religion, even Beyoncé is

a religion . . . what *isn't* a religion? Is everything a religion? If everything is a religion, might we also say that nothing is religion? Is "religion" a vacuous, even meaningless, term? How do we define "religion"? In fact, is it possible to define "religion" in the first place?

As we've seen, Marx based his definition of "religion" on Christianity, and a similarly Christian-centric conception of religion has persisted to this day. This is partly why many among the "spiritual but not religious" demographic in the West often identify themselves with Buddhism, which, as a nontheistic tradition without a Christian-style credal sense of orthodoxy or magisterium, does not appear to them as "religious" – even though there are certain forms of Buddhism that are formally institutionalized state religions in Southeast Asia. Similarly, here we see again why Marxism is sometimes described as a kind of "religion" with its vision of historical progress, culminating in the liberation of alienated workers into an ideal communist society – a narrative bearing a suspicious resemblance to Christian eschatology's vision of the redemption of an estranged and sinful humanity into the kingdom of God. So, though we may not know

Carlijn Kingma, *A History of the Utopian Tradition*, Chinese ink on paper, 2016.

what exactly are the essential features which make something a "religion," to describe any phenomenon as "religious" or as a "religion" is to say that it is something that *looks like* Christianity. When those who identify as "spiritual but not religious" so vehemently reject "religion," what they often mean is that they are skeptical of the institutionalism and dogmatism of organized religion associated with Christianity.

After all – "spiritual but not religious" and Christians alike – we often assume that we know what Christianity really is. Some people think of it as an aesthetic style (exemplified by the great artistic achievements of Baroque music, neoclassical architecture, and pre-photography painting); others a great books syllabus (often centered on Thomas Aquinas as the "culmination" of philosophical insights of Plato, Aristotle, Moses, and Jesus); still others a particular voting pattern or even an ethnic identity (most notably expressed in various forms of Christian nationalism). In all these cases and more, Christianity remains a religion – even *the* religion.

THIS QUASI-EQUATION between "Christianity" and "religion" may be helpful for understanding how the contemporary world has come to characterize and understand "religion" as a phenomenon – and why some people opt for "spirituality" instead. It may not be quite as helpful, however, in trying to understand what "Christianity" actually *is*.

Christianity was not always "*the* religion." It was originally a marginal position accused of being a form of atheism for its refusal to take part in worshiping Roman gods and the Roman emperor. Not only was Christianity a marginalized social movement, where Christians, as followers of Christ, were oppressed for deviating from Roman state paganism, it was a way of understanding reality that cut against the prevailing worldviews of the societies within which it first emerged. In other words, from a pagan perspective, Christianity didn't fit their idea of religion at all.

What Christianity introduced to Western thought was an account of what some scholars have called "post-heroic virtue." Unlike pre-Christian accounts of moral virtues and ethical ideals, the Christian vision of the good life neither celebrated heroic courage, prudence, and temperance as embodied by soldiers of Aristotelian excellence, nor did it exalt the pursuit of wisdom idealized in the Platonic philosopher who contemplates the good. The Christian moral vision is exemplified not by heroism but, as Christ taught in the Sermon on the Mount, by "the poor in spirit," "the meek," "the merciful," "those who mourn," the "peacemakers" who "hunger and thirst for righteousness" or "are persecuted because of righteousness." It is not the hero but the meek and humble – or as Saint Paul teaches, not the wise but those who, to the world, seem foolish – who embody what Christianity understands to be the good life or indeed, the *blessed* one.

Christianity was in its very origins a "critique of religion" itself, a way of living and thinking which called into question the dominant religious doctrines, moral systems, and the nexus of imperial power by throwing into doubt their assumptions about what it means to be a flourishing human.

The Christian affirmation of meekness or humility is not just a moral command but something that pertains to Christianity's very understanding of God. The Christian ethical call to "resist the proud and give grace to the humble" (1 Pet. 5:5), as Augustine observes in the *Confessions*, was exemplified by God in the Incarnation, wherein Jesus Christ, "despite being in the form of God, did not consider equality with God a thing to be grasped, but emptied himself and took on the form of a servant, made in the likeness of human form, humbling himself by becoming obedient to death – even death on a cross" (Phil. 2:6–8).

In the *Confessions*, Augustine notes that it is this radical emphasis on humility that most profoundly distinguishes Christianity from the philosophical and religious accounts of divinity found in rival worldviews, like that of Platonism. For Augustine, as for much of the Christian theological tradition, God's exemplification of humility and self-sacrifice in the Incarnation shows us one of the distinctive attributes of God held by Christianity: that God is love (1 John 3:16, 4:8). The Christian tradition holds, unlike Platonism and other rival worldviews, that God created the world out of *love*, as a free act of gift-giving, and not out of need or necessity. All that exists within the created order, including our very own being, is a gift from God.

True religion, then, is always a response to God – to God's generous, loving act of gift-giving. As Augustine writes in *The City of God*: "We offer to God the gifts God has given us, and the gift of ourselves. . . . This is the worship of God; this is true religion [*vera religio*]; this is the right kind of devotion; this is the service which is owed to God alone." *True* religion, for Augustine, consists not of adherence to particular moral precepts, doctrines, or institutions. Rather, it consists of "the worship of God," whereby we offer to God the gifts that God has given us, including what Augustine strikingly calls "the gift of ourselves." At the heart of "religion," in Augustine's portrayal, is what we might call *existential gratitude*: recognizing our existence as a gift given by God, that we are ourselves created as gifts of God, and that we are called to give to God "the gift of ourselves" – the gifts that we *are* – as an act of thanks-giving.

THIS ETHOS OF EXISTENTIAL GRATITUDE and thanksgiving is defined by humility: to acknowledge that our very own being *as* a gift requires us to accept that our existence is not something we deserve or something we are owed.

This isn't an easy thing to do. In our everyday lives, we often take our existence for granted. This is in part because the gift of existence is not as easy to recognize as other kinds of gifts are. Unlike things that are given to us as gifts at Christmas or birthdays, the gift of existence isn't something we can see or hear or taste; nor does it have a giver of this gift who is clearly visible to us (as our friends and family are). Yet many who are "spiritual but not religious" or even atheistic may say they are *grateful* for their existence, as if their existence is a gift given to them, even though they may not believe in a divine gift-giver to whom they feel grateful.

This "spiritual but not religious" attitude of existential gratitude is not about following certain rules or cultural conventions, nor is it about identifying oneself with a particular tribe or social group. It is, rather, as Robert Bellah memorably put it, a "habit of the heart." And from this kind of gratitude, Christians, perhaps, have something to learn. It's not just that the rejection of "religion" by the "spiritual but not religious" cautions us against the institutionalization and bureaucratization of Christianity: it challenges, or should challenge, our assumptions about the very nature of "religion" as a way of living and thinking.

Christianity is, as Augustine understood and Marx did not, at once a religion and a *critique of* religion. It calls into question the ways we have come to take the existing order of the world for granted by calling us to acknowledge that the things we have in this world – including our existence itself – are not possessions that we deserve. We are not to take these things for granted but to take them as gifts *granted to* us: gifts which invite a response in thanksgiving. Though the critique of religion may be the prerequisite of all critique, the prerequisite of true religion is not critique but the acknowledgment of the gift that we have been given.

Mother Mary in Cuba

After decades of Communist suppression of religion, I found marks of faith in my mother's hometown.

MARGARITA MOONEY CLAYTON

MY MOTHER WEPT SOFTLY as our plane landed in Havana. It was the summer of 1999, and I was in my early twenties, nearly the same age my mother had been when she was imprisoned by the Communist regime. She later fled to the United States, but the 1998 visit of Pope John Paul II to the island gave her the confidence to return for the first time since 1961. I remember being glued to the television as a vehemently anti-Communist Catholic pope from behind the Iron Curtain visited a nation that had once expelled priests and religious sisters, closed churches, and declared itself an atheist state in its constitution.

One of Pope John Paul II's stops was at the Shrine of Our Lady of Charity near Santiago de Cuba. The shrine commemorates Mary's appearance to three men, two indigenous and one enslaved, who nearly perished at sea in 1612. The three men prayed for protection from Mary and saw a vision of her. When they reached shore, a piece of wood bore Mary's image, inscribed with the words, "I am the Virgin of Charity."

A shrine was built for her at El Cobre, a copper mine on the island's eastern end, and has been expanded over time. Because El Cobre was the site where slaves in Cuba were granted freedom in 1801, Nuestra Señora de la Caridad del Cobre (Our Lady of Charity of the Copper Mine) became a symbol of freedom for the Cuban nation, especially during the fight for independence from Spain at the turn of the twentieth century.

Pope John Paul II's visit resulted in a slight loosening of the restrictions Cuba had placed on religious worship. Cuban exiles like my mother, who were previously banned by the Cuban government from visiting their homeland, were now allowed to come. The prospect of returning brought back horrible memories to my mother: she recalled being locked in a women's prison and hearing of executions. Several of her college classmates were shot by a firing squad. Her uncle was condemned to death but died of natural causes in prison before the sentence was carried out.

After landing in Havana, my mother and I drove through the beautiful countryside, searching for El Dolores, a sugar mill her family had operated in a village.

"There it is!" my mother exclaimed, pointing at a giant tower. "*El Ingenio Dolores.*" We drove along a road lined with palm trees and parked our Russian Lada near the *batey*, the village surrounding the sugar mill named for Our Lady of Sorrows, about an hour's drive from Havana.

Margarita Mooney Clayton is the founder and executive director of Scala Foundation, an associate professor of practical theology at Princeton Theological Seminary, and the author of When Mary Calls: Surprising Encounters with the Mother of God *(Odysseus Books, 2026), from which this essay is adapted.*

As we stepped out into the humid Cuban air that summer of 1999, my mother took a deep breath, savoring the scent of sugar being refined at the mill. The natural beauty was breathtaking; towering palm trees and the vibrant red leaves of a flamboyant tree welcomed us. The village remained practically unchanged – the only indicators of the passage of time were the dilapidation and abandonment of the same buildings that had stood there forty years earlier, including mostly small homes, an abandoned gas station, and a boarded-up church.

We were welcomed in the *batey* next to the sugar mill by villagers, one of whom carried the baptismal cards of my family members who had been baptized in the local church that they had built. With a big smile, she said, "I thought maybe you would return someday, and you might want to see these!"

After the Cuban Revolution, the church had been converted to a movie theater. Now the building stood vacant; its windows' empty frames covered with wooden panels. Inside, wild grass grew on the dirt floor. The few rays of light that streamed in flickered like candles.

We were taken to the house of one of the lay Catholics who had not abandoned his faith. Like many in Cuba, his backyard was filled with various knickknacks and random pieces of equipment. In a country where the economy had come to a standstill after the Soviet collapse, every object had potential uses. He smiled as he led us to something special, removing one wooden beam after another to uncover a large black tarp.

"*Las vitrinas!*" my mother exclaimed as the tarp was pulled back, revealing two stained glass windows from the church. We admired one window framed by roses. In the artwork, Mary held Jesus on her lap, surrounded by angels and shepherds who were worshiping him. The roses my mother had searched for were gone from the yard in front of her grandparents' house. Still, it seemed some roses had survived in people's hearts amidst the thorns of religious persecution.

The second stained glass window spared from the iconoclasm of the Communist revolution depicted Mary standing at the foot of the cross, her hands crossed, her eyes distressed, her heart wrenched with grief. Scripture tells us that Jesus cried out in anguish from the cross: "My God, my God, why hast thou forsaken me?" (Matt. 27:46).

Cubans at El Dolores had had no opportunities for Mass, confession, or sacraments for decades. Yet the slogans of the revolution had not erased the memory of fundamental Christian prayers. Groups met secretly to pray. In a land where the Bible was viewed as a tool for government subversion, the rosary, which consists of meditations on twenty scenes from scripture, served to preserve the memory of the faith.

The Cuban government had placed loyalty to socialism above all other ideals. The ruling Communist party had promoted atheism, closed many houses of worship, and discouraged public displays of religion. Yet the Cuban people remembered their spiritual mother.

The salty air and high winds eroded the triumphant faces of the then-still-living Fidel Castro and the long-dead Ernesto "Che" Guevara on walls and billboards across Cuba. Meanwhile, in private homes, I saw no images of Communist heroes. No one spoke of Castro or Guevara as if they were friends. Instead, Mary – depicted as Cuba's patroness and protectress, Our Lady of Charity – reigned inside Cuban homes. Time and again, people referred to Mary as someone close to them in their struggles.

Cubans' images of Mary at the foot of the cross were a rejection of the modern concepts that human progress is merely material and that our desire for communion with God is an illusion. Mary had lived through tumultuous violence; she was a mother who understood their fears and longing to keep faith alive through patience, lamentation, and hope.

One woman told my mother how, in desperation over her daughter's illness, she had prayed to Mary, but her daughter had not been healed. She tore a picture of Our Lady of Charity from a calendar on her wall and stomped on it. Not long after, her daughter was healed.

"Our Lady of Charity understands a mother's desperation when her child is suffering," my mother said.

My mother also visited a man whose son had died by suicide. In his living room, his wife lay catatonic while he recounted how his son had set himself on fire. The room's only decoration was a 1950s British motorcycle draped with two pictures of Our Lady of Charity. This family, engulfed by darkness, clung to the images of Our Lady of Charity as drowning souls might reach for a lifeline.

In another village where my mother had lived, we attended Mass at a church where the walls remained, though the roof had collapsed. A woman entered with flowers for the image of Our Lady of Charity. She told us she spent most of her time alone at home and had never set foot in a church before, yet she came into this roofless building to experience Mass for the first time. By bringing flowers to Mary, she made a tangible connection to an immaterial reality in which she placed her trust and hope.

After my seventh trip to Cuba, in 2005, this one alone, I drove to the airport in Santiago de Cuba with my friend Marcos. For two weeks, I had been distributing money, books, and religious items to political dissidents. On one occasion, after visiting a journalist documenting human rights abuses, I had been followed by the Cuban police, but I was not detained.

Now that I was departing, I raged against the abuses I had heard about from dissidents. Cuban Americans like me frequently wonder why those on the island don't resist the regime more. "Why don't people fight harder?" I asked Marcos.

"Margarita," Marcos replied gently, "you are about to board a plane. One hour later, you will be in Miami, taking a hot shower and enjoying a *café con leche*. If I could join you on that plane, I would. But I'm not allowed to leave Cuba."

His response humbled me. I was moved by the endurance and courage of those who were harassed and whose loved ones were jailed. People like Marcos, a medical doctor, adult convert to Christianity, and dedicated religious educator, performed daily acts of love and service, not demanding that God instantly relieve all their burdens, as I had.

"Somehow, in this atheist country, God granted me the gift of faith," Marcos continued. "I'm grateful to have found a community of love in the Catholic Church. After I drop you off, I'm going to visit an elderly woman who lives alone. I'll bring her some milk and spend time talking with her. You may not think I'm doing much, but this is the vocation God has called me to, and I will keep pursuing it."

His brotherly rebuke stirred my conscience. Resistance isn't always about grand gestures. Marcos reminded me that, like Mary at the foot of the cross, the steady presence that refuses to allow fear or hatred to prevail holds a power no government can stop.

As my plane lifted off from Cuban soil, I carried the deep imprint of lessons learned from Cuba's many public as well as quiet heroes. Their acts of courage, charity, and mercy showed me that the kingdom of heaven belongs not to those who combat injustice by dominating others, but to those who can remain steadfast in the darkness, trusting in a light that no earthly power can extinguish.

IN THE YEARS FOLLOWING my first visit to El Dolores with my mother, our family raised enough money in the United States to reopen the church. The beautiful stained glass windows were put back in place. Villagers had also hidden the *sagrario*, the tabernacle, where the blessed host is reserved.

Mary stands in those windows, surrounded by roses, holding the infant Jesus and staying with him at his cross. She remains there, not promising freedom from the cross or roses without thorns, but inviting people home to God, their father.

A few years after the church was rebuilt, the Cuban government dismantled the sugar mill of El Dolores. Piece by piece, the giant machinery that had operated for two centuries and sustained thousands of lives was gone.

But, my mother wrote, "God's house was standing restored. It stood there with the people after the sugar mill was gone, reminding everyone that God is with us, always in our need, and remains with us no matter what darkness."

During his 1998 visit, Pope John Paul II prayed at the Shrine of Our Lady of Charity that Mary would "gather together your peoples scattered throughout the world." The Cuban nation can only become "a home of brothers and sisters" through reconciliation rooted in self-giving love. Mary's title, Our Lady of Charity, he said, "evokes thoughts of the God who is Love" and "recalls the new commandment given by Jesus." Mary's "name and image are sculpted in the mind and heart of every Cuban, both within and outside the country, as a sign of hope and a focus of fraternal communion." Mary came "to visit our people and wished to remain with us as Mother and Lady of Cuba, throughout its pilgrimage along the paths of history."

In the secret rosaries prayed during decades of atheist rule, in the woman who brought flowers to a roofless church, in the villager who hid stained glass windows wrapped in a tarp and protected by wooden beams, I had witnessed how Mary's motherly love had helped prevent belief in God from being extinguished in Cuba.

Vera Jefferson, *Pear Orchard in the Moonlight*, oil on canvas, 2025

Pear Trees in Winter

To see the orchard stand undressed and cold,
shivering before the blue mountain, trunks dark
with winter fall, is to believe the old

tales of the winter gods. The darkened bark,
records the score of frosts since All Saint's Day,
but underneath the Christian year a stark

reality still lurks: the gods, the fay,
those cosmic psychos, that unstable lot,
those wisps of tricky light beside the way.

A door between the trees opens but not
because a house is there; it's not that kind
of door. Out come the winter gods you thought

were dead. Their slow parade begins to wind
between the darkened trunks. Now clutch your book
of prayers, thumb through the incensed pages, find

that psalm that burned you warm until you shook
the winter from your bones before. Take care
no glance falls on the wintered faces. Look

beyond the barren trunks. The frigid air
is split by stone and glass where faith gave birth
once to a hunkered chapel in the bare

field. Walk in. Look up. Wonder for all you're worth
to see there, high above, the humble stones of earth.

BENJAMIN P. MYERS

Knowing What Time It Is

What will our politics look like after Christianity?

JOHN EHRETT

Way back in the early 2000s, coming of age as a young conservative meant joining a sort of holy war. Ever since I could remember, faith and freedom and conservative politics had been wrapped up together in a seamless web. The terrorist attacks of September 11 stood for – in Samuel L. Huntington's famous formulation – a clash of civilizations, pitting Christian culture against an existential foreign threat. The New Atheists, Richard Dawkins and Christopher Hitchens and the rest, were a fifth column in the West betraying our Christian heritage. I can still recall sitting on my bunk at Summit Ministries' "worldview camp," poring closely over the pages of Ann Coulter's *Godless: The Church of Liberalism*.

This was the moral matrix – however faulty, flawed, and naive – that once formed the spine of

All photography by Yalim Vural.

American conservatism, at least as I remember it. But the web no longer hangs together so seamlessly. Moral concerns that once felt pressing – abortion and same-sex marriage, with drugs also in the mix – are decidedly marginal conservative talking points today. Newer issues, such as immigration, cultural cohesion, and domestic manufacturing of goods enjoy pride of place. There's overlap, of course – political leaders on the right still give the nod to Christianity, and the threat of radical Islam remains – but the sense of *theological urgency* has decidedly waned. We are well on our way, it would appear, to what the columnist and writer Ross Douthat has memorably described as the "post-religious right."

In June 2022, the *New York Times* published a lengthy guest essay chronicling this change, wondering quite explicitly, "What Comes After the Religious Right?" In its author Nate Hochman's telling, theological grammar no longer suffuses the political right, with its leaders no longer feeling pressure to invoke God or scripture in civic life. (In the wake of the Charlie Kirk assassination in September 2025, there was briefly an uptick in public theological language on the right, but that seems to be dying down.) According to Hochman, the leaders were responding to a voter base not particularly hostile to traditional belief, but not particularly drawn to it – yet *decidedly* opposed to any creed perceived as hectoring or moralistic. The new conservative coalition might be reflexively anti-progressive, but that did not make them faithful churchgoers.

Hochman left his reflections open-ended, musing that "while the old religious right will see much to like in the new cultural conservatism, they are partners, rather than leaders, in the coalition." But he concluded on a note of optimism: perhaps "the new cultural conservatism may protect the embattled minority of traditionalist Christians," even without restoring "them to their pre-eminent place in public life, as the old religious conservatism hoped to do." And, Hochman speculated, this new coalition – unlike the old Moral Majority – "may have an actual chance at winning." In many ways, it now has.

Hochman's essay evokes a particular narrative of religious decline – one in which, under the pressures of modernity, faith recedes from public life in Matthew Arnold's "melancholy, long, withdrawing roar." Left behind is a people that, over time, forgets that it has forgotten religion. The immanent world is felt to be sufficient to itself, driven by mundane concerns such as border policy and getting the bills paid on time. But the years since Hochman's essay suggest a different trajectory.

The essayist Wesley Yang once characterized the cluster of progressive ideas now widely described as "wokeness" as liberalism's "successor ideology" – a novel, relatively cohesive intellectual project that dare not speak its own name, lest self-definition trigger a backlash. What cannot be named, after all, cannot be coherently opposed. And yet that "successor ideology" was, in fact, something identifiable, and new.

Ample evidence now suggests that post-religious conservatism is producing its own "successor ideology." It manifests in divergent forms – from a technological maximalism that demands ever-greater transcendence of the body, to a primitivism fixated on physical strength, various imputed statistical differences between races, and (not quite ironically) phrenology. Its metrics are sets and reps, per capita statistics, and the marks on calipers. Its trajectories are complementary: they are grounded in a dawning conviction that *human politics and society are fundamentally defined by biology and its resultant*

John Ehrett is a Commonwealth Fellow at the Davenant Institute, a member of the Civitas political theology group at the Theopolis Institute, and a writer and attorney in Washington, DC.

hierarchies. Rebelling against the body's limits, or fixating upon them, both treat the body – rather than the immortal soul – as the primordial political term. And these moves follow organically from the dechristianization of the right.

The post-religious right will have its own creeds, however implicit. And it will inevitably find itself at odds with the Christian humanist tradition whose mantle it still claims.

BY WORLD-HISTORICAL STANDARDS, American conservatism has been strikingly egalitarian in character. To many, that claim may sound outrageous, given America's history of chattel slavery and mistreatment of Native American tribes. But by the standards of the left-right binary first formulated around the time of the French Revolution – with "left" meaning a taste for equality, and "right" an affinity for hierarchy – the American conservative experience looks decidedly nonhierarchical.

America imported no rigid system of social class from Europe. Its leaders did not, as in France, justify their rule by recourse to a sacred bloodline. Its founding authorities did not enshrine a metaphysical caste principle, along the lines of India's ancient Laws of Manu. But Americans who claim the mantle of "conservative" – a term of preservation and stewardship – cannot escape the reality that the American tradition they conserve is bound up with the Declaration of Independence's searing maxim: *We hold these truths to be self-evident, that all men are created equal, that they are endowed by their Creator with certain unalienable Rights, that among these are Life, Liberty, and the pursuit of Happiness.*

Just who are all these men who are created equal? For many in the founding generation, black Americans, Native Americans, and others didn't qualify. But attempts to enforce biopolitical hierarchies were always profoundly unstable. Whether consciously or not, slave owners were trapped in a paradox, committed to asserting the subhumanity of their slaves as the justification for their oppression while simultaneously living in perpetual fear of a freedom-seeking revolt – the very act of human self-determination epitomized by the Revolution itself. In time, and after much bloodshed, the logic of the Declaration won out. Those originally excluded from the American project of self-government on racial grounds proved entirely capable of being due, demanding, and receiving the rights enumerated in it.

The Declaration's logic, notwithstanding Thomas Jefferson's own dubious orthodoxy, is profoundly Christian in its orientation. The proclamation that *all men are created equal* is a decidedly transcendental claim, one that seems to defy the basic data of biology. After all, aren't some people stronger, and some weaker? Some beautiful, and others deformed? Yet they are equal in a more fundamental way: the undeveloped premise of Jefferson's argument is that, in their humanity, all people are equal relative to a Power beyond themselves, before whom all stand similarly dependent. As Lincoln would later put it, in an 1858 debate with Stephen Douglas:

> There is no reason in the world why the negro is not entitled to all the natural rights enumerated in the Declaration of Independence, the right to life, liberty, and the pursuit of happiness. I hold that he is as much entitled to these as the white man. . . . In the right to eat the bread, without the leave of anybody else, which his own hand earns, he is my equal and the equal of Judge Douglas, and the equal of every living man.

In recent years, some scholars have alleged that American conservatism – of all varieties – has always been racist to the core. They claim that familiar conservative values like limited government or religious freedom have all been fig leaves masking a deeper commitment to white supremacy. Racial animus, though, was never a facet of the conservatism with which I was raised. Growing up, we thrilled to the remarkable life story of Clarence Thomas, pored over the economic theories of Thomas Sowell, and celebrated the civil rights movement. Perhaps in one sense that was an end-of-history naiveté, masking the reality of unresolved questions. But we still thought that racial differences didn't count for much; such distinctions were always enfolded within a deeper common humanity before a Creator God. We understood that partisans of slavery and abolition alike had both looked to the Bible as an authority, but we didn't conclude that the Christian tradition was ultimately ambivalent on the question: a truly robust theological logic ultimately cut against biopolitical hierarchies.

TODAY, IT'S A MAINSTAY of some liberal commentary that Christianity is a reactionary creed, used to justify authoritarianism and oppression. But many genuine reactionaries have taken precisely the opposite view: Christianity embodies the sentimental, moralistic Western ethos they deplore. Friedrich Nietzsche's diatribes against Christian "slave morality" are the best-known versions of this critique, but they are nearly ubiquitous on the far right.

This criticism is not merely an attack on Christians' perceived pious detachment from the world. It is a root-and-branch challenge to the basic structure of Christian thought. In a certain sense, Christian faith *necessarily* levels and equalizes; by positing a transcendent God and a kingdom of heaven open to all, by positing a single human race descended from one pair of parents and made without exception in the image of one God, it unsettles claims to sacral kingship and renders any hypothetical biological inequalities irrelevant.

Far-right writer Sam Francis – who has recently enjoyed something of a renaissance among the online commentariat – went so far as to declare in a 2001 *Chronicles* essay that, because of its leveling and universalizing tendency, "Christianity today is the enemy of the West and the race that created it." And it was not only contemporary Christianity that he rejected: he regarded Christian anthropology in its original form as a delusion, its vision of transcendental justice and universal human value a hobble on the white race, preventing them from grasping the biological reality and material power that would bring America to his vision of greatness. "The religious orientation of the Christian Right," Francis argued in *Chronicles* in 1994,

> serves to create what Marxists like to call a "false consciousness" for Middle Americans, an ideology that appeals to and mobilizes a sociopolitical class but which does not accurately codify the interests and needs of the class and in the end only deflects its political action and works to buttress and reinforce the dominant regime.

This vision he shared, by his own account, with the majority of the figures on the pre-Buckleyite American Right: "Prior to World War II," Francis wrote,

> hardly any major figure on the American right was religious at all, and some were more or less outspoken enemies of religion in general and Christianity in particular. H. L. Mencken, Albert Jay Nock, and most of the group that Justin Raimondo identifies as the "Old Right" of the anti-New Deal, anti-interventionist orientation were not in the least concerned with religion except to mock it. Robert A. Taft, who generally shared the political views of this movement as he led its political efforts, himself seems to have lived and died as a thoroughly conventional Episcopalian, a calling almost indistinguishable from outright heathenism. The considerably less libertarian persuasion grouped around the racialist right, including Lothrop Stoddard and Madison Grant, was explicitly anti-Christian, while the "American fascist" Lawrence Dennis (as well as Ezra Pound) was also either uninterested in religion or hostile to it. Even in the 1950s,

the founder of the John Birch Society, Robert Welch, was a professed atheist and admirer of the Transcendentalist shaman Ralph Waldo Emerson, while Welch's one-time colleague, the late and brilliant Revilo P. Oliver, was as well-known for his bitterness toward what he called "Jesus juice" as he was for his animosity to Jews and their supposed conspiracy.

It is this Old Right that Francis missed, and that he sought to revive. That attempt was, in the decades in which the American right was guided by the Catholicism of William F. Buckley, the Evangelicalism of Billy Graham, and the mainline Protestantism of George H. W. Bush, unsuccessful. It had to wait for its time. That time, it seems, has come.

As I've previously written in these pages, the force of this right-wing attack is rooted in a straightforward claim: that "to live in accordance with the terms of Christian morality is to abandon other dimensions of human excellence altogether." This culminates in the further claim that biological difference is, in fact, meaningfully mediated *neither* by common descent *nor* common image-bearing *nor* ethnic-division-overcoming brotherhood in Christ. Such difference counts for a great deal, says the argument, so it's simply better for everyone to keep to his own kind, whether through geographic separation or (as Francis and some of his recent appropriators have advocated) a *de facto* racial dominance hierarchy.

In this view, Christianity's moral and metaphysical universalism is a ridiculous mythical straitjacket that arbitrarily restricts what can be done to preserve one's way of life. Better to be done with the contemptible idea of equality, and chase greatness instead.

THIS IS A NATURAL TRAJECTORY of "right-wing" – hierarchical – thought, shorn of a Christian mooring. Today, at the dawn of the post-religious right, that trajectory has become increasingly visible. Thus far, two distinct but complementary intellectual instincts have characterized the emerging post-Christian right. One might describe these as posthumanism and atavism.

In recent years, much has been made of the American tech sector's shift, at least rhetorically, to the right. Increasingly, pro-tech policies are justified through the language of national dynamism, risk-taking, and mastery, which echo common tropes of American conservatism. This repositioning is a natural extension of the industry's present trajectory: its engineers were never all that interested in DEI, but in charting new futures. And what new futures might those be? Elite billionaires now regularly speak of "life extension," but what kind? Judging by their remarks (and investments), many seem rather less interested in the survival of *human bodies* than in the survival of *human consciousness* – whether or not that consciousness is embodied.

Peter Thiel, the heterodox but professedly Christian venture capitalist and tech entrepreneur, has notably echoed these posthumanist themes in a recent series of lectures in which he argues for a drastically more technologically ambitious culture – he regards the present one as technologically stagnant, though he makes an exception for AI, in which he places a good deal of hope. Thiel's vision of Christianity and science bears a strong resemblance to the immortalist theology of Nikolai Fedorovich Fedorov, forerunner of the "Russian cosmist" philosophers who sought to bridge the gulf between science and mysticism.

Most famously, Fedorov argued that a quest for biological immortality – achieved through scientific means – was, in fact, at the esoteric heart of the Christian message. As Thiel remarked in a recent interview with Ross Douthat, this ambition has been shared by certain Western thinkers, including the seventeenth-century British statesman and philosopher Francis Bacon. Bacon was the author of the proto-science fiction novel *New Atlantis*, published posthumously in 1626, as well as works dedicated to promoting experimental science as the sole legitimate method of apprehending reality and improving the human condition.

Bacon saw man as interrogator of a reluctant nature. His overarching metaphor of scientific experimentation is, notoriously, the torture chamber, in which nature must be "wrought upon, and tortured, by human means," so that the experimenter may come to an overmastering understanding of nature which will allow him to command her:

> And that method of binding, torturing, or detaining, will prove the most effectual and expeditious, which makes use of Manacles and Fetters; that is, lays hold and works upon Matter in extremest Degrees.

According to Thiel, Bacon and later philosophers of science like Condorcet "thought we would have radical life extension. Immortality was part of the project of early modernity. . . . Maybe it was anti-Christian, maybe it was downstream of Christianity. It was competitive. If Christianity promised you a physical resurrection, science was not going to succeed unless it promised you the exact same thing."

Here, science and faith seem to coincide. But in Thiel's interpretation of the Christian promise, eternal life is not the province of God alone. Hope lies in technological progress – perhaps encouraged or directed by Providence, though he does not mention it, but fully taken in hand by man. Perhaps, just as Fedorov argued, human beings ought to undertake the "Common Task" of achieving immortality and godhood through technological accelerationism. Anything less than that is decadence, a dystopian anti-technological primitivism.

Thiel's vision of Christianity locates the classic Christian promise of resurrection and eternal life through God's grace – of the sharing in God's nature known as *theosis* – to the place where Bacon, Condorcet, and Fedorov looked for it: radical, species-altering technological progress. This is, in Thiel's view, the kind of cooperation with God to which humans are called – rather than the traditional Christian vision of a modest technological meliorism and the charge to tend the living world to bring it into greater fruitfulness in accord with its own nature and the sustaining will of God.

EVEN SO, THERE IS a critical difference between Thiel's worldview and Fedorov's "cosmism." As Fedorov would have it, the theological-scientific quest for immortality is grounded primarily in *duty to one's family.* Specifically, human beings are the agents *through whom* God would resurrect the dead of all generations – sons restoring their fathers, and so on back through the ages. As heterodox as it surely is (Fedorov avoided excommunication only by being very cautious about what he published, and his views have been declared heretical by his own Russian Orthodox confession), Fedorov's hope centered on human lives and bodies – and it was a hope fundamentally grounded in a duty that flowed from human nature itself.

But it is human nature which Thiel rejects – arguing, in his conversation with Douthat, that there was no Hebrew concept of human nature other than as fallen, as something to be overcome.

This is not the case. In a purely technical sense, φύσις, physis, the Greek "nature," is not used in the Hebrew Bible or in most of the Septuagint translation of those scriptures. (It is of course vividly and persistently present in the New Testament, which presumably Thiel would regard as authoritative.) The scholar T. C. Schmidt points out, however, that the idea represented by the Greek physis is present in many of the texts of the Old Testament. "Take, for example," he writes,

> the opening chapters of Genesis. . . . In Genesis 1:27 he makes humans according to his "image" (צֶלֶם) and "likeness" (דְּמוּת), humans who then go on to beget further humans in their "image," apparently passing on a divine stamp of what they should be, even if marred and broken.

This set of ideas shares a very large degree of overlap with physis, even in its technical philosophical sense.

Thiel casts off Fedorov's theological moorings in the service of something wholly novel – something deconstructive. He seems to be driven primarily by a sense that existing reality is so unacceptable that anything would be better, that we must commit ourselves to radical change brought about by technique, and it is not necessary to know what the end of that change will be. Is this really the work of God?

Douthat pushes him on this point: "Most of the people – present company excepted – working to build the hypothetical machine god don't think that they're cooperating with Yahweh, Jehovah, the Lord of Hosts." While Thiel agrees, he still seems to find it easier to make common cause with non-Christian tech visionaries than with Christians whose vision savors, one might say, more of Gandalf and less of Sauron. (In 2011, in an interview with Jonathan Miles in the magazine *Details*, Thiel discussed his love of *The Last Ringbearer*, Kirill Yeskov's novel that retells Tolkien's *Lord of the Rings* with Sauron as the hero: "Gandalf's the crazy person who wants to start a war," and "Mordor is this technological civilization based on reason and science. Outside of Mordor, it's all sort of mystical and environmental and nothing works.")

Thiel makes the point explicit. But similarly posthuman instincts are showing up among some on the right who might not view themselves as contributing to a post-Christian intellectual project, and might reject as heretical Thiel's formulation of the Christian promise of eternal life and of the sharing in the divine nature mentioned by Saint Peter. At a recent closed-door event I attended on AI policy, my co-panelist excitedly contended that AI development should remain largely unrestricted because the futures it promises are *inconceivable*.

That is a very peculiar word choice, with far-reaching implications. Technological futures should *always* be conceivable, in some fashion, because they begin from a standard reference point: human beings themselves, the users of technology. Envisioning and critiquing such futures has been the business of speculative-fiction writers for centuries, who repeatedly pose a critical question: *How will this technology affect human beings?* A technological future only becomes "inconceivable" when the basic reference point – human nature itself – becomes contestable. If our technological future is truly "inconceivable," it is only so because we have ceased to be recognizably human.

OR AT LEAST, some of us. Cryopreservation facilities, which hold bodies perpetually on ice in hopes of their later revivification (or the migration of minds into machines), are the province of the ultrarich. And there is no reason to assume that class divides will dissolve. If AI really does cause mass worker displacement, a two-tiered economic model seems inevitable: there will be those who own and advance the technology that does the work, and those living on a kind of dole.

In a posthuman age, the privileged few who escape the limits of the body, who evolve into *dei in machinis*, will find themselves immortal masters of the cosmos. Those unable or unwilling to undergo this evolution will be left behind. Here, traditional politics becomes pure biopolitics, the mastery of flesh over spirit. None of this is to imply that such a future is *possible* – from a Christian philosophical vantage, it isn't – but all that matters to direct political efforts toward it is that enough powerful people believe it can happen.

This underlying biopolitical instinct can also run in a superficially different – yet ultimately complementary – direction: toward an atavism willing to treat old markers of difference, like race and sex and (dis)ability, as politically determinative. The best-known atavist figure is, no doubt, Costin Alamariu, the formerly pseudonymous "Bronze Age Pervert." His 2018 book *Bronze Age Mindset* – inspired by his doctoral dissertation at Yale, later republished as *Selective Breeding and the Birth of Philosophy* – frames politics not as the pursuit of some common good but as a brute struggle for physical space.

Bronze Age Mindset's wry racialism is not a warrant for an immediate, organized fascist crusade, although that would be the political form Alamariu's plan would take if he thought it were possible. It is a harshly nontheological metaphysics to be adopted, he hopes, by readers for their personal use. Human beings are no more than evolved muck in motion, some possessing greater excellence: physical excellence, excellence perhaps in some emergent, immanent "life force." Those with the will and aptitude to do so should embrace the warrior spirit of the ancient Greeks, who – at least in the *Iliad* – seem to have no aspirations toward transcendent divinity, and instead embrace the pure pagan glories of immanence. But only a few are born with the natural physical and psychological capacities to thrive; the rest must be understood as, in his words, "biomass."

This biopolitical determinism informs vast swaths of what's often now called the "dissident right." It can be found in a fixation on "race and IQ" questions, which collapses human excellence into a single contingent term. It can be found in the obsession of the online "manosphere" with sexual "body counts"; here, one finds a frantic

urge to possess and retain, against all others, female bodies, to ensure that one's own bloodline is preserved. It can be found in ever-more-strident declarations that the American food system is corrupt and polluted, intentionally rendering the population sicker and weaker. (Never mind that agricultural technologies have prevented mass famines in non-Western countries; by an atavist account, the lives of non-Westerners comprise that biomass whose overgrowth they see as a sort of sickness on the planet.) Anti-Semitism, too, follows this logic. It's no coincidence that Jews have so often been maligned as "parasites" within the organic body of the nation – a decidedly biologizing metaphor if ever there was one. And of course it is from the Jews that we get the vexing notion that each man is made in the image of God, the irritating idea of the transcendent value of every human person.

Both posthuman and atavist currents flow from a common conviction: biology, whether we transcend it or reify it, is destiny. That conclusion follows from a rejection of Christian thought: in rejecting a genuinely transcendent Creator God, one removes the metaphysical predicate for Declaration-style pronouncements of human equality. *We are equal, relative to what?* It was the "freethinker" John Pettit, an Indiana senator and enemy of Lincoln, who in 1854, arguing for the extension of slavery to the Kansas-Nebraska territory, notoriously called the "self-evident truth" of human equality a "self-evident lie." It is, he argued, "not true that even all persons of the same race are created equal." Once that deletion is made, secular assertions of human equality become little more than mythmaking – at best, a noble lie; at worst, a psyop to hobble the strong. And in the face of statistical data and technological power, such myths are swiftly punctured.

Some Christians have found themselves tempted to ride the tiger of the post-Christian right. At least, the argument runs, *these folks recognize natural law. They recognize social order, if not moral order. That's a place to start.* Perhaps, too, these rightists might be valuable cobelligerents in a supposedly existential conflict with progressives.

This is a risky bet. For one thing, the "natural law" envisioned by such philosophies shares only a name with the natural law of, for example, Saint Thomas Aquinas, or even of Plato: it is the "natural law" by which the strong rule over the weak, not the natural law in which might must be in service to right, God's loving and self-giving nature, his reason, inscribed in ours. It is entirely possible – it is already happening in some quarters – that the ideological direction of travel will run in the other direction, with Christian theology being remade in ever more biopolitical ways, through the decontextualized retrieval of premodern texts. But such efforts at synthesis can only go so far. There is one battlefield upon which a traditional Christian ethic must finally collide, unavoidably and utterly, with the post-Christian right: bioethical questions of dependence and care.

Begin with natality. Plenty of tech icons have gestured toward the need for "pronatalism," a conscious endeavor to raise birth rates. But pronatalism comes in many forms. Viewed through a posthumanist, post-Christian lens, this quickly becomes eugenics: the selection of genetically optimized embryos and the destruction of the less fit. Simone and Malcolm Collins, part of the Thielite wing of the pronatalist movement, have argued that conceiving children via the old-fashioned and chancy process of intercourse is in fact morally wrong, and that all children should be conceived through in vitro fertilization with aggressive genetic screening and eugenic selection of embryos. This is, at this point, a relatively common approach, with companies such as Orchid running New York subway ads which offer boutique services focusing on IQ and other qualities prospective parents consider desirable.

There's another side of the coin: atavist logic supports widespread abortion. Why not decrease the surplus population of the genetically suboptimal? In the words of the Bronze Age Pervert himself: "Abortion should be mandatory in a number of cases: birth defects, rape, incest, miscegenation unless under approved aesthetic 'alchemical' combinations capped at certain percentages, parents' IQ less than ninety unless can prove countervailing advantage, and many other." His "classical" approach to eugenics reflects the practice, which he discusses extensively and approvingly in his doctoral dissertation, of the post-birth exposure of "unfit" infants. The older (and newer) Christian ethic – children as gifts of transcendent worth, knit together in their mothers' wombs, worthy of life and destined for union with God – can never reconcile itself to this, and has never been able to. Christians were, after all, known as those who unaccountably picked up those Roman infants exposed on hillsides, and raised them as their own.

An even more pressing clash is coming over the treatment of the elderly. Consider the facts: low birth rates in the Western world will lead to economies with fewer and fewer young workers and an ever-larger pool of retirees. Advancements in medical technology allow, in principle, for far greater longevity, even if radical life extension is still a long way off. But that care costs money – money that will come from the savings accounts, investments, and home equity of retirees, thus draining assets once handed down to the next generation. Those without assets will look to the state to provide – and, as a larger voting bloc than the younger working public, are likely to prevail.

This is a recipe for the widespread economic immiseration of the young: a sentence to work more and more, for less and less return, because their efforts must subsidize the care of the old. These conditions set the stage for the rapid mainstreaming of voluntary – or even involuntary – euthanasia of the elderly.

In his 1907 dystopian novel *Lord of the World*, the Catholic writer Robert Hugh Benson traces an end-times scenario following precisely this course. As Benson has it, the global faith propagated by the Antichrist is an immanent creed, centered on the value of humanity. Its ersatz godhead comprises the principles of "Maternity," "Life," "Sustenance," and "Paternity." And yet at the heart of the Antichrist's world order is a new clerisy, committed to a new sacrament of assisted suicide. Mabel, Benson's tragic protagonist, agonizes over "the taking of her own life, in a great despair with the world," seeing it as "an escape perfectly in accord with her morality." In the Antichrist's new order, "the useless and agonizing were put out of the world by common consent; the Euthanasia houses witnessed to it." In a post-Christian biopolitics, weakness is the unforgivable sin.

This logic perfectly – even uncannily – aligns with the biopolitical ethos of the post-Christian right, whether posthumanist or atavist. *Those who can pay to have their bodies frozen, their minds uploaded, let them. Why should the young and hale be sacrificed for the old and infirm?* None of this, as Benson foresaw, can be squared with Christian commitments – or for that matter, even older pre-Christian understandings of *pietas*, filial piety. No dissident-right Aeneas would bother to bear his father on his back: let old Anchises die, burned along with his defeated Troy, that the young one might found Rome. In a bitter irony, the progressive logic of absolute autonomy, and the post-Christian rightist logic of biological determinism, end up in the very same grave.

THE CHALLENGE of the post-Christian right is not that its ideas are incoherent and confused, born of healthy instincts which simply need to be channeled in a sounder theological direction. The challenge is that these ideas *are in fact deeply coherent* – and, taken together, represent a seductive alternative to a faith perceived as too anemic to withstand the coming technological and social storm.

Decades ago, Stanley Hauerwas memorably remarked that Christians will have done well if, in the centuries to come, they are known as "those peculiar people who don't kill their babies or their old people." For years, Hauerwas's comments have been invoked as a battle cry against secular humanism, against any progressivism that would deny the unique worth of human life.

But today, years on, there's a sharper edge to Hauerwas's words. The possibility that Christians may stand alone in the future – accepted by neither right nor left, a peculiar people indeed – no longer seems far-fetched. Any victory for "conservatism" won through forfeiting the Christian ethic of active love will prove a pyrrhic one.

There are other paths, and other strategies. Perhaps "knowing what time it is" means choosing life, and mercy, and the possibility of forgiveness. We can still choose to see, in the eyes and hands of all of those who share our nature, the image of God.

EASTEN LAW

The Church in China Isn't What You Think

A scholar dispels some common myths.

Plough *editor Joy Marie Clarkson sat down with Dr. Easten Law of South Korea's Yonsei University to discuss his research on today's church in China.*

Plough: Tell us about your research.

Easten Law: My research focuses on Christianity in contemporary China, and there's a very personal reason behind that. I am a second-generation Chinese American, born and raised in the United States. Though I spent many summers in Taiwan, it wasn't till college that my father took me to the People's Republic of China (PRC) for the first time, to further expand my cultural identity. After graduating, I spent some time in China teaching, worshiping at unregistered churches – often called house churches – as well as registered churches approved by the government. Experiencing worship and life in these churches

James Qi He, *Knocking at the Door,* Chinese ink on Korean paper, 1999.

raised many questions about what faith and religious life mean in a very different context.

I began my PhD studies with a simple question: How do young adult Chinese Christians practice their faith? That question grew into a broader one about how Chinese Christians negotiate their faith across cultures and borders. I'm eager to explore what the diversity of Chinese Christianity means for Chinese theology and the Chinese church.

Can you give us a beginner's history of the church in the People's Republic of China and how these churches are organized and perceived today?

The Chinese Communist Party (CCP) took control of the country in 1949. At first, the government didn't try to eliminate religion, but aimed to integrate it and create religious institutions that supported their broader communist goals. They established an ecclesial polity called the "Three-Self Patriotic Movement." "Three-Self" is an aspirational name that signifies a church that is self-governing, self-supporting, and self-propagating. In other words, a church that is free of foreign interference and, thereby, patriotically aligned with the vision of the Chinese government.

Of course, many churches refused to register with the Three-Self Church. They became what we now call unregistered or house churches. Generally, churches in China fall into one of two categories: registered or unregistered.

When the CCP decided to create a registered church, they tried to eliminate Western connections: the idea was to establish a Chinese church, not a church rooted in England or Germany or Rome. This is why the Three-Self Church refers to itself as "post-denominational." However, at the local level, many registered churches are aware of their denominational history. For example, they might know that before the establishment of the PRC, their congregation was Methodist.

The common view in China is that Roman Catholicism and Protestant Christianity are two separate religions because Protestant and Catholic missionaries didn't get along. As a result, Catholics have their own government-registered organization that is different from the Protestants'.

What are some Western misconceptions about the Chinese church?

One is that the Chinese church is constantly persecuted. When people have this impression, they're actually thinking about different periods in modern China's history – the original effort was to consolidate rather than to persecute.

But many churches refused to comply with the Communist Party. Once you reach the Cultural Revolution around the 1970s, you see the Party shift toward trying to eliminate religion. By then, it didn't matter if a church was registered or not; they sought to end religion altogether. It was a particularly intense and significant moment.

Interestingly, during the later period of economic reform in the 1980s, when China opened itself to the world, a sense of religious revival also emerged; the party loosened its grip and allowed churches to rebuild. The registered church was rebuilt, and house churches were more public than ever before. Sure, they didn't own buildings or have signs that said "there's a church here," but the government was very open to them continuing to meet.

Even unregistered churches would rent out entire floors of office buildings or hotels, and many nonregistered Christians would gather to worship, while the government turned a blind eye. There was a social understanding that if you kept to yourself and contributed positively to society,

---

Dr. Easten Law is an incoming faculty member at Yonsei University's United Graduate School of Theology and its Global Institute of Theology in South Korea. He previously served as the associate director of the Overseas Ministry Study Center at Princeton Theological Seminary.

it was acceptable. During the 2000s through 2010s, these unregistered house churches became quite visible. They opened Christian bookstores, operated nonprofits to serve communities, and started elder-care centers. Local governments appreciated this because there was a shared belief that churches helped maintain social harmony.

But by 2013, when Xi Jinping stepped into power, we began to see that tightening again. Many unregistered churches are now feeling increased pressure. Not to the same extremes as during the Cultural Revolution, but churches are being shut down, and leaders are being arrested.

Is there a consensus about whether the church is growing? Or how big it is?

The short answer to your question is no; it's impossible to get an exact number. The official government figures tend to be on the low side; higher estimates suggest around 10 percent of the population is Christian. However, based on my research, I would lean toward a figure in the middle, roughly 5 percent.

Both demographers and scholars of Chinese Christianity currently believe growth is beginning to level off. After China opened up in the nineties and its economy started to flourish, people became wealthier. Along with this, there was a yearning for spiritual fulfillment because the economic boom led to a wild west of trade and capitalism, making morals seem lax, and people sought a spiritual center. During this period, Christianity experienced a significant surge. Interestingly, it's not just Christianity that grew; people revisited Buddhism, Daoism, and a variety of other spiritualities to find stability. But now we're seeing a slight flattening in religious growth.

How has the Chinese government responded to Christianity's growth and this return to religions more broadly?

In response to this return to faith and spirituality, the government has launched a campaign to "Sinicize" religions, to adapt faith traditions to Chinese culture. This is somewhat absurd in some cases: how can you make Daoism, an indigenous Chinese tradition, more Chinese than it already is? When the government talks about Sinicizing religion, they mean making it more communist or socialist. It's as if they decided, "We've allowed religion to flourish, but now it's time to bring it back in line." While unregistered churches face traditional persecution – leaders being arrested; churches shut down – registered churches must theologize very carefully, often in dialogue with, and sometimes in strict submission to, what the Party dictates Christian theology should be.

There's an abiding myth that registered churches are just tools of the Communist Party, that they do whatever it demands. I want to clarify that this isn't true.

The registered church has always played this game. There's an abiding myth that registered churches are just tools of the Communist Party, that they do whatever it demands. I want to clarify that this isn't true. Many in the registered churches are genuine Christians. They simply have a different perspective on church and state, and they choose to navigate this relationship with the Party. They will sign the necessary documents. They will give speeches, such as on the Sinicization of Christianity. But they also take care of their congregations and try to help people walk in faith. Their approach to negotiation with this tightening

control is different from that of house churches, which are resisting, hiding, and moving around.

Are there breaking points at which registered churches won't be able to continue submitting to the Party?

I'm confident that some church leaders are very frustrated, but the reality is that you won't hear this publicly expressed. It's simply not possible. China has developed a security system, especially since Covid, that rivals the best in the world. They use surveillance on a level that many countries cannot match. Today, there are cameras everywhere in China, along with facial recognition technology. During Covid, they introduced systems that allowed them to track your location via your phone. This technology has significantly strengthened China's control over free speech during the past decade. Chinese Christians are very aware that what they say or think could be used against them at any time. It's a very challenging time for freedom of speech for everyone in the country.

How can a Christian in the West help or pray for the Chinese church?

The good news is that with every wave of tightening or persecution, the Chinese church has learned to adapt and grow in faith – so much so that they don't rely on the West. They don't need outside churches to support their spiritual lives; they've found ways to support and grow with each other. I would say that one hears about a need for theological education. There's always a sense that

James Qi He, *Calling Disciples,* Chinese ink on Korean paper, 1999.

About the artist: James Qi He grew up during the Cultural Revolution in China. As a young man, having taken some art lessons, he began painting portraits of Mao Zedong in order to avoid field labor. One day he saw Rafael's painting of *Madonna and Child* in an old art magazine. He was drawn immediately to the peace of the scene, and this led to his interest in Christianity. He studied medieval art at the Hamburg Art Institute in Germany and then went on to receive his doctorate in Religious Art from the Nanjing Art Institute in 1992. His particular interest is in depicting biblical stories from a culturally Chinese perspective. His work is a unique blend of medieval European artistic influences and Chinese folk art.

Chinese churches need to train more pastors and teachers.

The Chinese continue to be influential global players in many areas, from building physical infrastructure, where Chinese workers are employed on construction sites worldwide, to education, with students attending top schools. For instance, in the United Kingdom, there are many Chinese residents, especially following events in Hong Kong over the past few years.

One of the best things churches around the world can do, as China globalizes, is to be a witness through their hospitality to Chinese expats and migrants, whether they're elite Chinese studying or laborers working on highways, and regardless of the political dynamics between their nations. That's the way to create strong global relationships. The Chinese people are dynamic, negotiating all kinds of questions about faith and spirituality and power – the Chinese people are not the Chinese government. If the church in other parts of the world can truly be hospitable and welcoming, it will mean building relationships with the Chinese people.

How has this sense of the global Chinese church shaped your faith?

When I look at the diversity of Chinese churches around the world, I think about how the Holy Spirit sanctifies us in many ways, including migration and awareness of migration for those who may not experience it directly. Even for someone born and raised in South West England, or someone in the American Midwest, if you go back a few generations, your family did move. We've all moved at some point. That awareness of how God is present to us wherever we are – individually and as families, across multiple generations – feels deeply biblical and very formative. I try to embrace this spirituality of migration, the idea that God has been faithful to me and my family across generations and through movement. Through this lens, I find that the whole Bible makes more sense to me.

You can look at the migrations in Genesis, in the books of the prophets, the migration of the church in the New Testament. God is present with those who are moving, and it's in the moving that we draw closer to God. It's in the moving that we become more Christlike. This has helped me develop what I call a migratory consciousness. We talk about historical consciousness – migratory consciousness is a part of that, I suppose. Knowing that we have all been migrants, if not physically, then spiritually and emotionally, just moving through seasons of life. And that's how God shapes us, right? The more we become aware of it, the deeper the Spirit can work in us.

This interview was conducted on November 18, 2025, and has been edited for length and clarity.

Pascal's Night of Fire

What distinguishes a believer from a cultural Christian?

GRAHAM TOMLIN

On a cold November night in 1654, a young Frenchman, well known in fashionable circles for his scientific experiments and mathematical genius, sat down to pray in his small apartment in Paris. What happened next surprised him. For about two hours, he had an extraordinary experience of the presence of God, which turned his life around and set him on a new trajectory.

The man was Blaise Pascal. He told no one of this experience, but wrote an account of it which he hid in the lining of his jacket. It was found by chance by a servant preparing his body for burial when he died eight years later. The document became known as the *Mémorial* and the event as Pascal's "Night of Fire."

"God of Abraham, God of Isaac, God of Jacob – not of philosophers and scholars."

—Blaise Pascal

The term "cultural Christianity" has become prominent recently, notably when the public atheist Richard Dawkins described himself as a "cultural Christian." He claims to enjoy Christmas carols and church architecture, despite not believing a word of Christian doctrine – recognizing, as he put it, "a distinction between being a believing Christian and being a cultural Christian."

Before his Night of Fire, Pascal was by no means an atheist like Dawkins, or even a mere cultural Christian. He had a faith, yet it did not penetrate to the core of his soul in the way it did afterward. Looking again at the text of the *Mémorial* can help us navigate what Christianity might look like in a world after religion: cultural Christianity may be a starting point, a good thing in itself, but must not be confused with real, personal Christian faith. So, in a Western world where Christians have become a minority, what is the difference between what Dawkins calls a cultural Christian and a believing Christian?

A Habit of Prayer

The first thing apparent in Pascal's new intensity of faith is an instinct to pray. His description of his experience begins:

> "God of Abraham, God of Isaac,
> God of Jacob"—
> not of philosophers and scholars.
> Certainty, certainty, heartfelt, joy, peace.
> God of Jesus Christ.
> My God and your God.

The whole account is in the form of a prayer. Pascal's is an encounter, not with the God of the philosophers, the divine architect of the universe, a God at the end of a logical argument, but the God of Jesus Christ, who, as C. S. Lewis once put it, is "alive, pulling at the other end of the cord, approaching at an infinite speed, the hunter, king, husband."

Pascal can do nothing other than worship this God who brings him "joy, joy, joy, tears of joy." His theological mentor was the great Saint Augustine, who taught that faith begins when God's grace kindles a desire for him within the hearts of human beings, and this is exactly what Pascal experienced. It led him to a life marked till its end by regular patterns of worship and prayer.

One of the crucial differences between the cultural Christian and a believing Christian is the development of the discipline and habit of prayer. A cultural Christian might admire Christian values and ethics, even argue for them in political life, but does not feel the need to embark on the

---

Graham Tomlin is the author of many books, most recently Blaise Pascal: The Man Who Made the Modern World *(Hodder, 2025), and a former Bishop of Kensington. He is editor in chief of* SeenandUnseen.com.

Evan Rosa, *Illustration of Pascal as a figure of mystery, mechanics, faith, and modern technological influence*, digital illustration, 2025.

highly personal business of prayer.

Pascal's Night of Fire was over within two hours. It didn't last – such experiences never can. Yet he carried the memory of it close to his heart, allowing it to shape his priorities, his use of time, the focus of his attention. For the rest of his days he reoriented himself not so much around his scientific and mathematical explorations but around a life of spiritual devotion. He continued with his scientific work, but it became less central to his identity. Pascal was aware that his scholarship held within it the temptation to pride and the desire for praise, with the spiritual dangers inherent there. Now his focus was on worship.

True faith involves a searing honesty about the despair that lurks in our own hearts.

Spiritual Sickness

Such experiences happen to some Christians but not all. I'm not sure I have experienced anything similar, and many Christians I know would say the same. Yet there is another part of Pascal's encounter that is a mark of all true Christian experience: Pascal describes experiencing his own shame. "I have cut myself off from him, shunned him, denied him, crucified him."

Amidst the ecstasy of encountering divine love comes this profound sense of inadequacy, of ignominy – not to put too fine a point on it, of sin. Pascal is aware of the abyss within his own soul, the shallowness of his life, the way he has ignored the God on whom his life depends, and how he has wasted God's gifts.

Some time ago I listened to a conversation between Richard Dawkins and Ayaan Hirsi Ali, a former Muslim fundamentalist turned hardcore atheist. She had recently announced her conversion to Christianity. Dawkins assumed that her conversion was to a genteel cultural Christianity like his, but as she told her story it gradually dawned on him that something deeper had taken place. Hirsi Ali described an episode of prolonged suicidal depression, which no psychological treatment or scientific reasoning had helped. A therapist diagnosed her problem not as mental or physical but spiritual, suggesting she might even try praying. When she did, she began, mysteriously, to encounter the same God that Pascal had.

Dawkins was incredulous that Hirsi Ali had started to believe ridiculous things like the Incarnation, the Virgin Birth, and the Resurrection. Reluctantly, he had to admit that it sounded like she was a proper Christian. The nub of the issue for Dawkins was his objection to the idea of sin. It was, he said, "obvious nonsense. . . . The idea that humanity is born in sin, and has to be cured of sin by Jesus being crucified . . . is a morally very unpleasant idea."

Of course it's unpleasant. Crucifixions were. From the perspective of those who have no sense whatsoever that they need saving, it is distasteful, embarrassing, not the kind of thing that you bring up in Oxford Senior Common Rooms. I too find unpleasant the notion that I am sinful, stubborn, deeply flawed, in desperate need of forgiveness and healing. I would much rather think I am fine as I am. Yet there are many things that are unpleasant but necessary. Like surgery. Or changing dirty diapers. Or having to admit addiction.

And that was ultimately the difference between Dawkins and Hirsi Ali. They were each as clever as the other; they had both read the same books; they knew the same people. Yet Hirsi Ali, like Pascal, had been to a place where she knew she needed help, a help that no human being could provide, whereas Dawkins, it seems, had not.

This is the second factor that marks out real from cultural Christianity. The cultural Christian has little sense of having a spiritual sickness that needs healing, has not looked into the abyss, or owned his part in the darkness of humanity, and has no notion of needing any kind of salvation. True faith involves a searing honesty about the despair that lurks in our own hearts, the self-centeredness that plagues our lives, our society, and our politics. It knows we cannot solve it ourselves.

An Urge to Share

An immediate outcome of Pascal's Night of Fire was a new project, which took on a greater significance than his scientific or mathematical work. At the time, as a celebrated figure in Parisian intellectual life, he was surrounded by sophisticated people interested in gambling, hunting, games of tennis, impressing everyone with their witty conversation – nominal Catholics and cultural Christians who, when it got down to it, found God boring. Pascal immediately began to think about how he might persuade them they would find true happiness not in their trivial entertainments but in God himself.

So he started to write what he intended as a great apology for the Christian faith, addressed to these skeptical friends of his, scribbling down ideas that came to him from time to time. Some were just a line, some a few paragraphs, some like longer essays. He never finished his apology. When he died aged just thirty-nine, his friends found the notes he had left behind, eventually publishing them as his "thoughts" – Pascal's *Pensées*.

This desire that others find faith is a third mark of true Christian belief. Lesslie Newbigin, the great scholar of missions, who encountered Western culture afresh when he returned in the 1970s from decades of missionary service in India, used to say that "mission is the test of our faith." How can you tell whether someone really believes that Christ is the unique son of God, that he died for the sins of the world, that he rose again as a foretaste of the new creation to which the entire world is headed? The crucial test is a willingness to make that belief public. Speaking of the gospel, Newbigin wrote: "We believe that these events are the real clue to the story of every person, for every human life is part of the whole human story and cannot be understood apart from that story. It follows that the test of our real belief is our readiness to share it with all peoples."

The cultural Christian might see evangelism as a kind of cultural imperialism and shy away from any attempt to share the faith with others. Yet the deeper faith goes into our hearts, the more profound our experience of both joy and shame:

Pascal's is an encounter, not with the God at the end of a logical argument, but the God of Jesus Christ.

the unique combination that the gospel brings to human experience. The more we believe Christianity to be true, the more we will desire that others discover it. Of course, this doesn't mean that all true Christians are rabid evangelists or apologists, or disrespectful of the wisdom found within other faith traditions; they simply desire that others discover what they have, and they seek sensitively to use whatever gifts they have to commend that faith in public.

A Spirit of Sacrifice

The other major impact of the Night of Fire was its inspiration of Pascal's new desire to serve and to share his life sacrificially with the poor. He began to give away many of his possessions, to live a simpler life, even taking a homeless family into his apartment. He expressed a desire to die among the poor because they were the ones with whom Christ spent his time. "I love poverty because

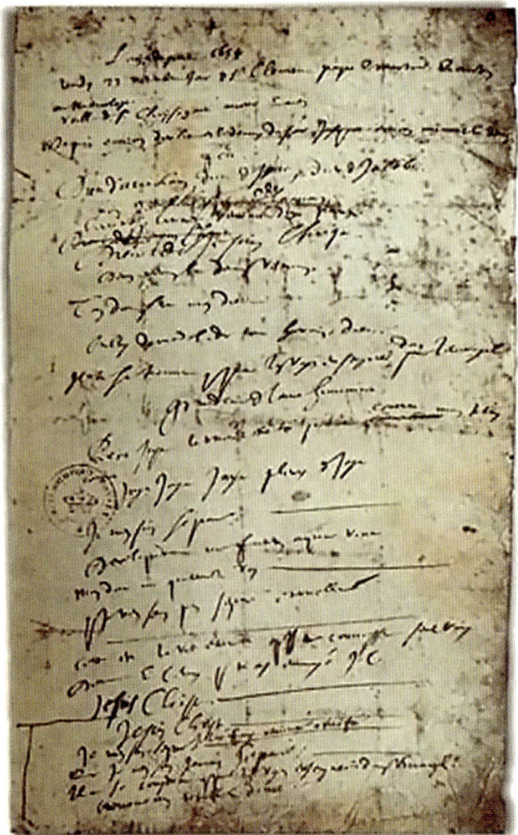

[Christ] loved it," he wrote. "I love wealth because it affords me the means of helping the needy." It led him to use his entrepreneurial ingenuity to come up with the first urban public transportation system in Europe, a fleet of coaches envisioned specifically to enable poor people to travel the greater distances required in the expanding city of Paris, at minimal cost.

Alan Kreider's book *The Patient Ferment of the Early Church* describes "the improbable rise of Christianity in the Roman Empire." Kreider shows that for the early Christians, care for the poor was one of the key tests of true faith. Before being baptized, catechumens were asked about their use of money and whether they could show evidence of having supported the poor, especially among the Christian community. One of the factors that marked out Christians from others in the late empire was their willingness to visit the sick and give to the poor in a society where gifts were usually calibrated to win favor and advantage.

Of course, as Tom Holland's book *Dominion* has pointed out, the early Christian belief in care for the poor, because each person is made in God's image, has become secularized by now

> **An instinct to pray, a deep sense of sin, a desire to share the treasure of faith, and sacrificial involvement in the lives of the poor are clear signs of authentic Christian life.**

into a general belief in charitable action, even if the Christian grounding for it has been forgotten. Yet the example of the early Christians, and of Pascal, shows that a mark of true faith is not only financial generosity to the poor but the willingness to build relationships with them. It is a willingness to sacrifice your own wealth or time in a way that sees the purpose of life not as pleasure or consumption but as love. Today, the problem is not so much that the rich don't give to the poor, but that the rich don't know the poor. True Christian faith costs. It means involvement in the life of those who struggle at the tough end of an unequal society.

Pascal's Night of Fire and its impact help us discern what marks out the life of a believing Christian, especially in a post-Christian world. An instinct to pray, a deep sense of sin, a desire for others to discover and share the treasure of faith, and sacrificial involvement in the lives of the poor are clear signs of authentic Christian faith and life.

Blaise Pascal's *Mémorial*, 1654.

Clarence Gagnon, *Trees in the Sun*, 1903

Afterwords

High summer throbs and buzzes like a light
bulb burning out, the fields all full of wings.
I walk through hum and chaffing, keep my sight
set on a surging through the heart of things.
Grass shoots through concrete walkway somehow, green
breaking up gray. In hardness, where to root?
This everyday I walk a path between
earth, sky, and deeper earth. More than a suit
for ghost, my body also hopes to rise.
A white horse runs through pasture in my dream,
its mane a rippling mirror of the sky's
own clouds. Like clay, I'm mostly what I seem,
a little not. I'd stroll this grassy hill
forever, if I could, and often think I will.

BENJAMIN P. MYERS

FERN HILL
by DYLAN THOMAS
NOW AS I WAS YOUNG AND EASY UNDER THE APPLE BOUGHS
ABOUT THE LILTING HOUSE AND HAPPY AS THE GRASS WAS GREEN,
THE NIGHT ABOVE THE DINGLE STARRY,
TIME LET ME HAIL AND CLIMB
GOLDEN IN THE HEYDAYS OF HIS EYES,

***Julian Peters** is the author of* Poems to See By *(Plough, 2020) and* Nature Poems to See By *(Plough, 2026), which includes this poetry comic. He lives in Montreal, Canada.*
***Dylan Thomas** (1914–1953) was a Welsh poet and writer.*

AND AS I WAS GREEN AND CAREFREE, FAMOUS AMONG THE BARNS
ABOUT THE HAPPY YARD AND SINGING AS THE FARM WAS HOME,
IN THE SUN THAT IS YOUNG ONCE ONLY,
TIME LET ME PLAY AND BE GOLDEN IN THE MERCY OF HIS MEANS,
AND GREEN AND GOLDEN I WAS HUNTSMAN AND HERDSMAN, THE CALVES
SANG TO MY HORN, THE FOXES ON THE HILLS BARKED CLEAR AND COLD,
AND THE SABBATH RANG SLOWLY
IN THE PEBBLES OF THE HOLY STREAMS.

ALL THE SUN LONG IT WAS RUNNING, IT WAS LOVELY, THE HAY
FIELDS HIGH AS THE HOUSE, THE TUNES FROM THE CHIMNEYS, IT WAS AIR
AND PLAYING, LOVELY AND WATERY
AND FIRE GREEN AS GRASS.
AND NIGHTLY UNDER THE SIMPLE STARS
AS I RODE TO SLEEP THE OWLS WERE BEARING THE FARM AWAY,
ALL THE MOON LONG I HEARD, BLESSED AMONG STABLES, THE NIGHTJARS
FLYING WITH THE RICKS, AND THE HORSES
FLASHING INTO THE DARK.

AND THEN TO AWAKE, AND THE FARM, LIKE A WANDERER WHITE
WITH THE DEW, COME BACK, THE COCK ON HIS SHOULDER: IT WAS ALL
SHINING, IT WAS ADAM AND MAIDEN,
THE SKY GATHERED AGAIN
AND THE SUN GREW ROUND THAT VERY DAY.
SO IT MUST HAVE BEEN AFTER THE BIRTH OF THE SIMPLE LIGHT
IN THE FIRST, SPINNING PLACE, THE SPELLBOUND HORSES WALKING WARM
OUT OF THE WHINNYING GREEN STABLE
ON TO THE FIELDS OF PRAISE.

AND HONOURED AMONG FOXES AND PHEASANTS BY THE GAY HOUSE
UNDER THE NEW MADE CLOUDS AND HAPPY AS THE HEART WAS LONG,
IN THE SUN BORN OVER AND OVER,
I RAN MY HEEDLESS WAYS,
MY WISHES RACED THROUGH THE HOUSE HIGH HAY
AND NOTHING I CARED, AT MY SKY BLUE TRADES, THAT TIME ALLOWS
IN ALL HIS TUNEFUL TURNING SO FEW AND SUCH MORNING SONGS
BEFORE THE CHILDREN GREEN AND GOLDEN
FOLLOW HIM OUT OF GRACE,

NOTHING I CARED, IN THE LAMB WHITE DAYS, THAT TIME WOULD TAKE ME
UP TO THE SWALLOW THRONGED LOFT BY THE SHADOW OF MY HAND,
IN THE MOON THAT IS ALWAYS RISING,
NOR THAT RIDING TO SLEEP
I SHOULD HEAR HIM FLY WITH THE HIGH FIELDS
AND WAKE TO THE FARM FOREVER FLED FROM THE CHILDLESS LAND.
OH AS I WAS YOUNG AND EASY IN THE MERCY OF HIS MEANS,
TIME HELD ME GREEN AND DYING

THOUGH I SANG
IN MY CHAINS
LIKE THE SEA.

Poems to See By: A Comic Artist Interprets Great Poetry
Julian Peters

A fresh twist on 24 classics, these visual interpretations by comic artist Julian Peters will change the way you see the world.

This stunning anthology of favorite poems visually interpreted by comic artist Julian Peters breathes new life into some of the greatest English-language poets of the nineteenth and twentieth centuries. Grouping unexpected pairings of poems around themes such as family, identity, creativity, time, mortality, and nature, *Poems to See By* will also help young readers see themselves differently. Includes poems by Emily Dickinson, Langston Hughes, Carl Sandburg, Maya Angelou, Seamus Heaney, e. e. cummings, Robert Frost, Dylan Thomas, Christina Rossetti, William Wordsworth, Robert Hayden, Edgar Allan Poe, Percy Bysshe Shelley, John Philip Johnson, W. B. Yeats, Gerard Manley Hopkins, Edna St. Vincent Millay, and Siegfried Sassoon.

Hardcover | 160 pages | ~~$26.00~~ $18.20 with 30% discount for subscribers. Use code PQ30 at checkout.

Nature Poems to See By: A Comic Artist Interprets More Great Poetry
Julian Peters

Kirkus Most Anticipated YA Books of Spring 2026

These are poems that can change the way we see the environment, and encountering them in graphic form promises to change the way we read the poems. This sequel to Peters' first book includes adaptations of poems by Langston Hughes, William Shakespeare, Sylvia Plath, Emily Dickinson, Gerard Manley Hopkins, William Wordsworth, Mary Karr, Robert Frost, Edward Thomas, William Blake, Dylan Thomas, Robert Burns, Rhina P. Espaillat, Joy Harjo, Alfred L. Tennyson, Matsuo Bashō, Gwendolyn Brooks, Stevie Smith, Li Po, Carl Sandburg, e. e. cummings, Elizabeth Bishop, and Philip Larkin.

Hardcover | 152 pages | ~~$29.95~~ $20.97 with 30% discount for subscribers. Use code PQ30 at checkout.

Plough Short Fiction Contest

We're looking for original short stories
that honor the mysterious nature of reality
and find transcendence and redemption
in unexpected places.

First prize $2000

For more information, visit *plough.com/fictioncontest.*

Editors' Picks

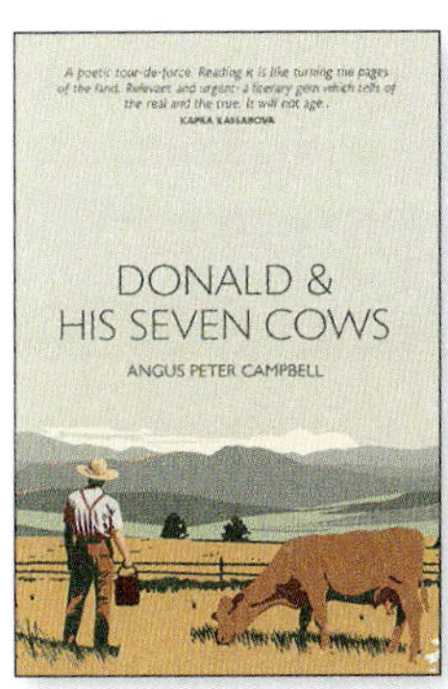

Donald and His Seven Cows

By Angus Peter Campbell
(Luath, 208 pages)

I almost didn't finish *Donald and His Seven Cows* by Angus Peter Campbell. It's not badly written. In fact, it reads cleanly and naturally, and the prose has a rhythm that feels authentic. At the same time, at least on the surface, it's a book about a solitary old farmer on a Scottish island who spends all day taking his cows for walks and listening to the fairies. A good novel opens the door to a brand-new world and invites you in. Initially I didn't want to go.

In the end, it was the lucid, childlike chatter of the narrator, Donald, that drew me in to a grudging curiosity, followed by real enjoyment. Why was he nattering on about his lead cow, Maisie? What is the significance of plodding around the same mile of pasture every day? To the reader, Donald's life appears to be one of failure: missed opportunities, lack of ambition, stifled romance, and unutterably boring loneliness. Donald, however, seems to be at peace with the world, contented. He's an odd one. His neighbors call him a fool and think he may be coming adrift mentally.

Donald spends all day with his cows, leading them on a "round mile" and stopping to graze at twelve marked intervals. There is an allusion to the Stations of the Cross in this. The book is a one-way conversation with the reader as Donald goes around, meditating on his life, his cows, his neighbors, faith, relationships, and the change and loss of community that he has witnessed through his life. Interspersed throughout are a number of folktales related to the landscape. Donald talks to his cows, to folktale characters, and to the people of his past. And they talk back to him. The use of Gaelic words and expressions is charming.

> It's a joy to have all these voices from elsewhere join those of Maisie and the herd and *Mac Talla nan Creag* and Catrìona as we walk the round mile together. I think of how big a world lots of little things make. Like how I make my porridge every morning from a handful of pinhead oats and milk and watch how it bubbles up and swells to fill the pan and my plate and my belly. One thing becomes another.

The reader is kept in suspense on the subject of Donald's sanity. Is he imagining his conversations with the landscape, or does he really believe they are happening? But then, how sane is modern life, where many conversations take place online with people one has never met?

At the novel's end, Donald is compelled to make a decision about what sort of life he wishes to have: the comfort of living in splendor or the real life he has with his cows. There's even a sweet little love interest.

This is a book about faith, and meaning, and reality. The lines that have stuck with me are these:

> I don't believe in God because I've seen miracles or because it comforts me but because he's as real to me as the wellington boots I stand in. He's everywhere, from the gurgling sound my tea makes as I pour into my cup first thing every morning to the wild way the wind sweeps against the gable end of the house every night. The miracle is that I can lie down to sleep every night and get up every morning believing it's worth getting up again. To stir the fire and boil the kettle and feed Wilhelmina and Rover and to greet Maisie and the herd, again and again, for our new day's adventure.

—Ian Barth

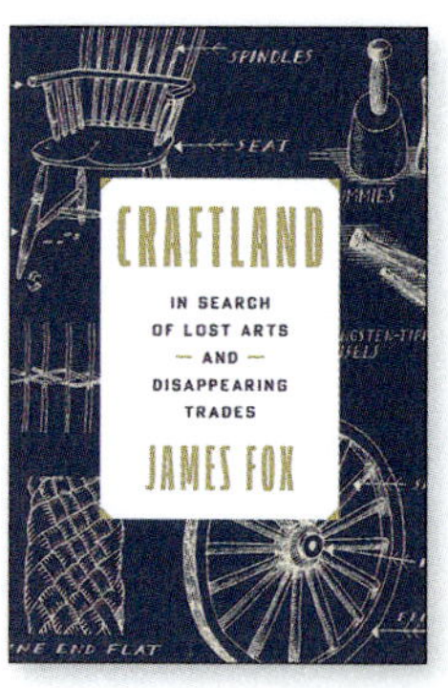

Craftland

In Search of Lost Arts and Disappearing Trades

By James Fox
(Crown, 368 pages)

Since I moved up to the Yorkshire Dales, the drystone walls that criss-cross the valley pastures and fell tops have become an ever-present feature of my new northern life. Many of these beautiful walls are hundreds of years old and have borne the brunt of the worst the northern weather can throw at them. They are thus often in need of repair. This is no simple task. It calls for a certain kind of laborer: one who is well-versed in age-old practical knowledge and whose tactile instincts have become so well trained that he knows exactly what shape and size of rock is required to complete the three-dimensional puzzle confronting him.

Drystone wallers are among the hundreds of traditional craftsmen still plying their trades across Britain and are the first that James Fox, an art historian at Emmanuel College Cambridge, visits on his tour of endangered crafts in his book *Craftland*. Fox meets the men and women responsible for crafting some of the United Kingdoms' most loved and beautiful creations: thatched cottages in the Scottish Highlands, Windsor chairs in the Chilterns, and the church bells that ring across the nation. Each craftsman is characterized by a single-minded devotion to his trade, a commitment to defending handworking methods from modern efficiency and automation, and a deep affection for the tools, many of which have been passed down from generation to generation.

One thing that becomes clear throughout the book is that many of the traditional crafts, in contrast to industrialism, are in harmony with nature. Fox visits willow-coppice workers and reed harvesters who sustainably utilize local natural resources at rates that allow nature to recover. Further, in an age where wildlife is so often made homeless by human development, many of the crafts provide homes for creatures, such as voles and mice sheltering inside the crevices of the lichen-encrusted drystone walls. We see in this harmony a glimpse of how humanity's work was meant to be back in Eden – work that benefits the whole community of creation, people and creatures alike.

All is not well, though, with the crafts. Fox wishes to alert us to a tragedy. Many traditional crafts are becoming extinct as they are outcompeted by modern industries or as their last practitioners retire or die without an apprentice to whom to hand over the reins. There were a few poignant moments where Fox traveled to interview a craftsman only to arrive a day or two after he had died – his skills perishing along with him. Whenever this happens a part of the nation's soul is lost. Traditional crafts "are part of who we are and where we come from. They connect us to our ancestors and our local communities, weaving the past with present, forging collective identities, shaping our immediate surroundings."

Though many crafts have been lost and many more are threatened with extinction, Fox ends on a hopeful note. If we learn to value the crafts again, viewing them not only as luxuries or hobbies but as an essential part of our societies, the future might be one where the crafts and craftsmen thrive. It will be a world where many more of us enjoy the pleasure of holding in our hands beautiful products made with skill, love, and wisdom, and which display, in their little imperfections, the unmistakable marks of a human touch.

—Hadden Turner

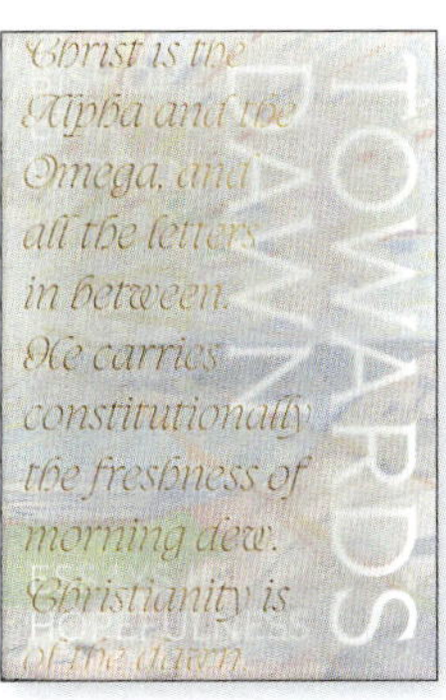

Towards Dawn

Essays in Hopefulness

By Erik Varden
(Word on Fire, 160 pages)

Bishop Erik Varden of Norway lives in the past. As a Trappist monk and former abbot, he follows an ancient rule and held a position of leadership in an order with roots stretching back a millennium. He studies dead languages and popularizes the third- and fourth-century teachings of the Desert Fathers. In his writing, he makes casual reference to obscure black and white films, old operas, poems, and fairy tales. And yet, at a recent speaking engagement, this Bishop of Trondheim, Norway – a medium-sized city six hours' drive from Oslo – was introduced as "a man who knows what time it is."

As the subtitle of his recently published essay collection, *Towards Dawn*, suggests, now is a time for hope, a stance not easily supported by the headlines. There are some hopeful signs in America, France, and the United Kingdom of a spiritual revival stirring, and in Varden's native Norway, where belief in God is a minority position, the small Catholic population is increasing. But these glimpses of dawn come after decades of secularization, disaffiliation, and disestablishment in Norway and around the world. Twenty years have not passed since Charles Taylor published *A Secular Age*, and lawmakers daily challenge believers' deepest convictions. But for Varden, terms such as "post-Christian" are incoherent, they make "no sense" theologically, for "[Christ] carries constitutionally the freshness of morning dew. Christianity is of the dawn."

Towards Dawn is a short book, comprised of ten essays. The first is the most programmatic, including Varden's model for engagement with culture. The most memorable is the third, which features Varden's discussion of yoga. He relays the story of a Belgian monk and medievalist who took up, then popularized, what came to be known as "Christian yoga." The monk recovered medieval debates over the relationship between the body and soul and put the Christian theological tradition into conversation with the rising tide of interest in Eastern religions. Varden jumps off from this moment to draw out lost physical manifestations of Christian practice: bodily ascesis, fasting, the regulation of appetites. From there comes the principle that "the state of one's body is not indifferent to the state of one's soul."

Varden plays the English language like an instrument, and his essays are too individually rich to sort into a narrative or rhetorical arc. They are not sociological, although he is concerned with trends, especially among the young, nor are they strictly theological, although they are dense with theology. Varden's essays feel more spiritual, concerning the spirit of Christian hope, defined unconventionally as the "confidence that everything, even suffering, disappointment, and injustice, can be purposeful." Through hope, one moves toward Christ, light, truth, and dawn. His method is to take an unexpected subject – like a Holocaust memoir or DEI policies – and use it as a hermeneutic key to unlock his intended object. In one of his previous books, he used such "keys" as Wagner's *Triston and Isolde* and the apocryphal *The Book of the Cave of Treasures* to get at the true meaning of chastity. Varden's use of juxtaposition would wear thin were he not so earnest. One gets the sense that an essay stripped of poetry and allusion would be inauthentic to the man.

—Jacob Akey

How Solzhenitsyn Found Faith

GARY SAUL MORSON

"Gradually it was disclosed to me that the line separating good and evil passes not through states, nor between classes, nor political parties – but right through every human heart."

—Aleksandr Solzhenitsyn

DOSTOYEVSKY CHOSE JOHN 12:24 as the epigraph to *The Brothers Karamazov*: "Verily, verily, I say unto you, except a corn of wheat fall into the ground and die, it abideth alone: but if it die, it bringeth forth much fruit." Suffering enables one to reach the deepest truths. An episode from Dostoyevsky's own life, familiar to his contemporary readers, illustrates this point: As punishment for illegal political activities, he was condemned to be shot – but then was pardoned at the last possible moment and imprisoned for four years in a czarist prison camp. In those extreme conditions Dostoyevsky found faith, and his story became exemplary for other Russian sufferers.

The gulag to which Aleksandr Solzhenitsyn was sentenced in 1945 was incalculably worse than any czarist prison camp. His famous history of the gulag prison camp system, *The Gulag Archipelago*, shocked Western readers who had had only a vague idea of how horrible that system was. It made the czarist prison camps, described by Dostoyevsky in his *The House of the Dead*, look like a vacation resort by comparison. And yet those extreme conditions led Solzhenitsyn and some others to look inward and find faith. For the epigraph to Part IV of *The Gulag Archipelago* ("The Soul and Barbed Wire"), he selected 1 Corinthians 15:51: "Behold, I shew you a mystery; we shall not all sleep, but we shall all be changed." Prison changed Solzhenitsyn. As he tells the story, it led him from self-congratulatory materialism to repentance and faith.

The Gulag Archipelago, written in the 1950s and '60s and published in 1973, is, among other things, the story of Solzhenitsyn's journey from atheism to God. Describing the many ways people were first arrested (your date arrests you at the end of a lovely evening; you are taken unconscious from the operating table), then interrogated under torture (lowered naked into boiling oil; having your testicles slowly compressed), transported to Siberia (in railroad carriages so densely packed that some prisoners are suspended above the ground between others), punished (by hard labor at fifty degrees below zero), and subjected to unrelenting hunger for years on end – at each example of what an arrested person undergoes, Solzhenitsyn pauses to recount his own experience. Yet for all the depredations, his story turned out to be a happy one – he insisted on this – because it led him to understand life's meaning and purpose. He ends the book's central chapter, "The Ascent": "*Bless you, prison*, for having been in my life!"

TRAINING TO BE AN OFFICER in World War II, Solzhenitsyn came to regard himself as superior to ordinary people. Anticipating an officer's stars, students "developed a tigerlike stride and a metallic voice of command," which became habitual. Years later Solzhenitsyn recalled how, only a month after "the officer's stars were fastened" on him, he had abused a careless soldier. "And do you know, I had *forgotten* all about it until now. . . . Only now, seated in front of this sheet of paper, have I remembered. . . . Pride grows in the human heart like lard on a pig."

With horror, Solzhenitsyn remembered how he had tossed out commands he would allow no one to question, "convinced that no orders could be wiser. Even at the front, where, one might have thought, death made equals of us all, my power soon convinced me that I was a superior human being." Addressing old men with condescending familiarity, he "sent them out to repair wires under shellfire so that my superiors should not reproach me." One of them even died that way. Like a pre-revolutionary aristocrat, Solzhenitsyn

---

Gary Saul Morson is an American literary critic and scholar best known for his work on Leo Tolstoy and Fyodor Dostoyevsky. He is Lawrence B. Dumas Professor of the Arts and Humanities at Northwestern University.

was served by an orderly. "That's what shoulder boards do to a human being. And where have all the exhortations of [my] grandmother, standing before an ikon, gone!"

"Had I at least kept my student's love of freedom," it would not have been so bad, "but, you see, we never had any such thing. Instead, we loved forming up. . . . I remember very well that right after officer candidate school I experienced the *happiness of simplification*, of . . . *not having to think things through* . . . the happiness of forgetting some of the spiritual subtleties inculcated since childhood." Echoing Dostoyevsky, he notes that people love to escape from responsibility by acting as the agent of some theory or institution. It gives them what Mikhail Bakhtin called a spurious "alibi for being." The official term for this in Soviet education was "partyness," the virtue of not thinking for oneself but following without question those who, according to Marxist-Leninist ideology, had the indubitable truth.

Even when Solzhenitsyn was arrested in early 1945 for criticizing Stalin in a letter to a friend, his attitude did not change. "There was more than enough time to consider my former life and to comprehend my present one. But I couldn't." Even as he was led away, he made someone else carry his bag because he, after all, was an officer. Had someone accused him of haughtiness, "I would *not have understood* him!"

Although Solzhenitsyn came to regard Stalin as a gangster, he, like many others, at first remained a devoted Marxist-Leninist. He told another prisoner "that our Revolution was magnificent and just. . . . I said there had been a long period in which the people in charge of everything important in our country had been people of unimpeachably lofty intentions." So devoted was he to Lenin that when someone called another prisoner, the pre-revolutionary radical Fastenko, by Lenin's patronymic, asking "'Ilyich, is it your turn to take out the latrine bucket?' – I was utterly outraged and offended because it seemed sacrilege to me not only to use Lenin's patronymic in the same sentence as 'latrine bucket,' but even to call anyone on earth 'Ilyich' except that one man, Lenin." Fastenko instructed: "'Thou shalt not make unto thee any graven image!' But I failed to understand him! . . . One thing is absolutely definite: not everything that enters our ears penetrates our consciousness. Anything too far out of tune with our attitude is lost."

TO GROW WISER, Solzhenitsyn had to learn, in defiance of all his education, to think for himself. In this respect, he resembled Innokenty Volodin, a character in his novel *The First Circle* (1968). Volodin, a Soviet ministry official, has always read only books "warranted sound," so that all he had to do was absorb what they said. When he discovers his mother's pre-revolutionary diaries and books, Volodin must learn something new: how to read while questioning. Solzhenitsyn, too, had to give up the comfort of "simplification" and appreciate complexity and doubt. Colonel Vorotyntsev, the hero of Solzhenitsyn's series of novels *The Red Wheel*, set during World War I, comes to understand that such questioning demands a kind of courage very different from that required to face enemy bullets without flinching. Thinking for oneself demands the courage to be alone with one's beliefs and to maintain them even against the pressure to conform.

The key moment came when the imprisoned Solzhenitsyn met three young people who had defied shared opinion. When he remarked matter-of-factly that a recently published prayer from President Franklin D. Roosevelt had of course been hypocritical, one of them, Boris Gammerov, turned on him in fury: "Why? Why do you not admit the possibility that a political leader might sincerely believe in God?"

> And that is all that was said! . . . I could have replied to him very firmly, but prison had already undermined my certainty, and the principal thing

Previous spread, clockwise from top left: Lithuanian deportee house in Kolyma region, 1958; Aleksandr Solzhenitsyn in exile in Kazakhstan, 1953; Gulag prisoners working on a small railway in the Komi Republic.

"At the time I was committed to that world outlook which is incapable of admitting any new fact or evaluating any new opinion before a label has been found for it from the already available stock."

—Aleksandr Solzhenitsyn

> was that some kind of clean, pure feeling does live within us, existing apart from all our convictions, and right then it dawned upon me that I had not spoken out of conviction but because the idea had been implanted in me from outside.

"Implanted from outside": Solzhenitsyn realized that he did not believe what he thought he believed. His political convictions were not the product of his own thought, and therefore, however sincerely he might express them, they were something alien. This realization testified to something within him that was deeper than he had suspected. Evidently, "some kind of clean, pure feeling does live within us, existing apart from all our convictions." Of course, Solzhenitsyn could have suppressed this insight, and he had probably done so before. But what he saw in prison gave him pause.

Gammerov and his friends continued to challenge Solzhenitsyn. "At the time I was committed to that world outlook which is incapable of admitting any new fact or evaluating any new opinion before a label has been found for it from the already available stock: be it the 'hesitant duplicity of the petty bourgeoisie,' or the 'militant nihilism of the déclassé intelligentsia.'" Now Solzhenitsyn was pressed to change not just his particular beliefs but also his understanding of what it means to hold beliefs at all. He had to learn to entertain the possibility that evidence or logic might lead him to change his mind. Marxism-Leninism claimed to be not just true but the very standard of truth, so that anything that contradicted it was by definition wrong. Solzhenitsyn had to reject this view before he could reject any of Marxism-Leninism's specific theses.

When Solzhenitsyn at last appreciated the value of diverse opinions, he entered a period of radical skepticism. Nerzhin, the autobiographical hero of *The First Circle*, resembles, in the words of one of his Marxist friends, a "young Montaigne" and an "infant Pyrrhonist" – which is to say, he personifies doubt, and, like Solzhenitsyn himself, he comes to regard prison as a blessing: "It's made me think."

Nerzhin grasps the limitations of human reason. As someone tells him, "Writers try to explain people completely, but in real life we never get to know anyone completely. That's why I love Dostoyevsky. . . . The closer you get [to his characters], the less you understand them." Solzhenitsyn strove to make his own characters just as elusive.

When another prisoner confides his plan to overthrow the regime and set up a better one, Nerzhin answers that, even if this scheme were feasible, it might make things even worse, just as the overthrow of repressive czarism had done. "I simply don't believe that anything good and durable can be constructed on this earth of ours," he explains. "How can I set about advising you when I can't disentangle myself from my own doubts?"

Nerzhin realizes, however, that radical doubt is not enough – that its destructive power is useful but that it lacks the power to build – and he grows skeptical of skepticism itself. Just as there are no atheists in the trenches, there are no relativists in the frozen gulag. “However clever and ungainsayable such philosophical systems as skepticism . . . may be,” he observes, “you must remember that they are in their very nature condemned to impotence.” For life to be meaningful, it is necessary to “affirm something.”

Nerzhin is deeply moved by the religious prisoner Kondrashov, who insists that ethics are not entirely relative to the class structure of society (“being determines consciousness”), and that people are not infinitely malleable, as the Party maintains. “Every man is born with a sort of inner essence,” Kondrashov asserts. “It is, so to speak, the innermost core of the man, his essential self. No ‘being’ . . . can determine him. Moreover, every man contains within himself an image of perfection, which . . . sometimes stands out with remarkable clarity! And reminds him of his chivalrous duty!”

Don’t laugh at the medieval idea of chivalry, Kondrashov continues. “In the days of chivalry, there were no concentration camps! No gas chambers!” It turns out that Kondrashov, a painter who has produced bad official art, has secretly painted his own ideal of perfection: the moment when Parsifal first catches sight of the Holy Grail. In it, a gray horse emerges from a forest and stands before an abyss:

> The rider himself had no eyes for the abyss. . . . He was staring in rapt amazement, into the depths of the picture, where an orange-gold radiance suffused the whole expanse of the sky above, emanating perhaps from the sun, perhaps from a still purer source. . . . Stepped and turreted, growing out of the stepped mountain and visible also from below through the cleft between the cliffs, between the trees and the ferns, rising to a needle point in mid-heaven at the top of the picture, hazy and indistinct, as if spun from shifting cloud, yet discernible in all the details of its unearthly perfection, ringed in a blue-gray aureole by the invisible supersun, stood the Castle of the Holy Grail.

What led Solzhenitsyn to his own chivalrous struggle and subverted his skepticism was the Soviet theory of ethics, which he recognized as fundamentally wrong. Objective morality, according to the official view, is a myth perpetrated by the ruling classes to keep others in subjection. Morality is always class-based and so entirely relative. Reading his mother’s diaries, Volodin, the ministry bureaucrat, is amazed that she and her friends “in all seriousness . . . began certain words with capital letters – Truth, Goodness, Beauty, Good and Evil, the Ethical Imperative. In the language used by Volodin and those around him, words were more concrete and easier to understand – progressiveness, humanity, dedication, purposefulness.”

Volodin’s mother believed in compassion and pity, as if they were objective virtues somehow inscribed in the skies, rather than relative to particular classes. Soviet doctrine, by contrast, taught that compassion for class enemies is a vice, and cruelty practiced by the Party a virtue. The word “conscience” fell out of use, replaced by “consciousness” (as in “class consciousness”).

For Lenin, materialism ruled out any idea of objective goodness. Such an idea could derive only from God or from philosophical idealism, which

Gulag prisoners transporting goods along the Izhma River, 1930.

was simply disguised religion. The only goodness, from a Leninist perspective, is expediency – that is, whatever serves the interests of the Party. As Solzhenitsyn describes it in *Gulag*, Soviet children were taught the fundamental lesson that, for a materialist, the material result is all that counts.

> It is important to forge a fighting Party! And to seize power! And to hold on to power! And to remove all enemies! And to conquer in pig iron and steel! And to launch rockets! And though for this industry and for these rockets it was necessary to sacrifice the way of life, and the integrity of the family, and the spiritual health of the people, and the very soul of our fields and forests – to hell with them! The result is what counts!!!

If it is necessary to arrest people not for what they did but for what they might do ("we protect ourselves . . . against the future"), and if it is expedient to starve millions of peasants to death in order to collectivize agriculture, and if it is useful to deport whole nationalities to Siberian wastes where most will die: well, it is the result that counts!

Citing the common belief that between 1918 and 1920, the secret police "did not shoot all those condemned to death but fed some of them alive to the animals in the city zoos," Solzhenitsyn argues that although he does not know if the rumor is true, one can be sure that, according to official ideology, there is no reason to regard such an action as immoral. After all, "How else could they get food for the zoos in these famine years? Take it away from the working class? Those enemies were going to die anyway, so why couldn't their deaths support the zoo economy of the Republic and thereby assist our march into the future? Wasn't it *expedient*?"

Recognizing that atheism and materialism, taken to their logical extremes, lead to this morality, which his deepest self rejected, Solzhenitsyn realized that somewhere inside he really did have faith. He recalled how he and some other students had once been invited to join the secret police. Everything he believed (or thought he believed) told him this move would be not only personally advantageous but also morally upright, and yet for some reason he could not explain, he could not do it.

> It was not our minds that resisted but something inside our breasts. People can shout at you from all sides: "You must!" And your own head can be saying also: "You must!" But inside your breast there is a sense of revulsion, repudiation. I don't want to. *It makes me feel sick.* Do what you want without me; I want no part of it.

And so the faith of his ancestors survived within him: "Without even knowing it ourselves, we were ransomed by the small change in copper that was left from the golden coins our great-grandfathers had expended, at a time when morality was not considered relative and when the distinction between good and evil was very simply perceived by the heart."

All the same, Solzhenitsyn also recalled, he could have been persuaded to join the secret police, and so it was only chance that he did not become a torturer. There but for the grace of

Convicts building a camp near the Eastern Siberian Railway.

Spiritual rebirth happens only if, faced with the gulag's fundamental choice, the prisoner chooses rightly: one must decide whether to survive at any price, even if to do so, one causes another's death.

God go I! He therefore had no claim to moral superiority, all the more so because, as an officer, he had given needless orders that led to the deaths of others. "So let the reader who expects this book to be [only] a political exposé slam its covers shut right now." The book is more than that. It is also a personal confession, the story of how, bit by bit, he recognized his own sinfulness and recovered the faith he did not know he had.

IT HAS LONG BEEN KNOWN, Solzhenitsyn observes, that prison can cause "the profound rebirth of a human being," although more often it doesn't. Spiritual rebirth happens only if, faced with the gulag's fundamental choice, the prisoner chooses rightly: one must decide whether to survive *at any price*, even if to do so, one causes another's death. "This is the great fork of camp life. From this point the roads go to the right and to the left. One of them will rise and the other will descend. If you go to the right – you lose your life, and if you go to the left – you lose your conscience."

When prominent Bolsheviks found themselves arrested, they invariably made the wrong choice. After all, they were just applying the maxim "the result is what counts" to their own cases. The people who behaved best were the religious believers, an observation we can trust because we find it even in the memoirs of those who, like Evgeniya Ginzburg, remained Marxists and atheists. "In the course of this book," Solzhenitsyn comments,

> we have already mentioned [the believers'] self-confident procession through the Archipelago – a sort of silent religious procession with invisible candles. How some among them were mowed down by machine guns and those next in line continued their march. A steadfastness unheard of in the twentieth century! And it was not in the least for show, and there weren't any declamations.

Atheist officials treated these "nuns," as believing women were called, with special vindictiveness. They were "kept only with prostitutes and thieves at penalty camps. And yet who was there among the religious believers whose soul was corrupted? They died – most certainly, but . . . they were not corrupted." Reflecting on such displays of courage, Solzhenitsyn concluded: "It is not the result that counts! It is not the result – but *the spirit!*"

Achieving faith required one more step: one must squarely face one's own sinfulness. So long as one treats oneself as a victim of others' injustice, one remains "sharply intolerant" and judgmental. Tolstoy's novels and stories make the same point: to become enlightened, one must recognize the evil in one's own heart, face the sins one has committed but arranged to forget, and consider how easily one might have been led to even worse ones. Solzhenitsyn advises: "Reconsider all your

> **"Yes, you have been imprisoned for nothing. You have nothing to repent of before the state and its laws. But . . . before your own conscience?"**
>
> —Aleksandr Solzhenitsyn

previous life. Remember everything you did that was bad and shameful and take thought. . . . Yes, you have been imprisoned for nothing. You have nothing to repent of before the state and its laws. But . . . before your own conscience?"

Solzhenitsyn recalled how, as he lay alone in the surgical ward of a camp hospital, a Dr. Boris Kornfeld spoke with him and described his own conversion to Christianity. "On the whole," Kornfeld confided, "I have become convinced that there is no punishment that comes to us in this life on earth which is undeserved. Superficially it can have nothing to do with what we are guilty of in actual fact, but if you go over your life with a fine-tooth comb and ponder it deeply, you will always be able to hunt down that transgression of yours for which you have now received this blow."

That night, Kornfeld was murdered in his bed, and so, Solzhenitsyn realized, these words were his last. "And, directed to me, they lay upon me as an inheritance. You cannot brush off that kind of inheritance by shrugging your shoulders." They struck Solzhenitsyn because he had already entertained similar thoughts. He decided that Kornfeld's ideas were not quite right because they seemed to indicate that the innocent people who suffered at the hands of the Nazis and Bolsheviks must have been "some sort of super evildoers" to deserve such punishment. All the same, "there was something in Kornfeld's last words that touched a sensitive chord, and that I accept quite completely *for myself.* And many will accept the same for themselves."

As he lay there for many nights in the surgical ward, Solzhenitsyn "pondered with astonishment my own life and the turns it had taken." To remember his thoughts, he set them down in verse. When he was younger, he recalls:

> Bookish subtleties sparkled brightly,
> Piercing my arrogant brain,
> The secrets of the world were . . . in my grasp. . . .
>
> But passing here between being and nothingness,
> Stumbling and clutching at the edge,
> I look behind me with a grateful tremor
> Upon the life that I have lived.
>
> Not with good judgment nor with desire
> Are its twists and turns illumined.
> But with the even glow of the Higher Meaning
> Which became apparent to me only later on.
>
> And now with measuring cup returned to me,
> Scooping up the living water,
> God of the Universe! I believe again!
> Though I renounced You, You were with me!

Reviewing his life, Solzhenitsyn grasped that what he had regarded as beneficial "turned out in actuality to be fatal, and I had been striving to go in the opposite direction to that which was truly necessary to me." His suffering taught him "this essential experience: *how* a human being becomes evil and *how* good." When he thought he was doing good, that was precisely when he was doing the most evil. In *The Gulag Archipelago*'s most famous lines, he confides:

> And it was only when I lay there on rotting prison straw that I sensed within myself the first stirrings of good. Gradually it was disclosed to me that the line separating good and evil passes not through states, nor between classes, nor between political parties either – but right through every human heart – and through all human hearts. This line shifts. Inside us, it oscillates with the years. And even within hearts overwhelmed by evil, one small bridgehead of good is retained. And even in the best of hearts, there remains . . . an unuprooted small corner of evil.

"The falsehood of all the revolutions in history" has relied on making the opposite assumption: that the line separating good and evil lies between groups, and so it is only necessary to separate and eliminate the evil people. Those who do so "take to themselves as their heritage the actual evil itself, magnified still more."

But "all the religions of the world" struggle instead with "the *evil inside a human being* (inside every human being). It is impossible to expel evil from the world in its entirety, but it is possible to constrict it within each person," beginning within oneself. To do so, we must engage in (as Solzhenitsyn put it elsewhere) "repentance and self-limitation." Solzhenitsyn found faith when he appreciated the evil in his own heart. We must all do the same.

SOLZHENITSYN EXTENDED his idea of repentance and self-limitation to Russia as a whole. Because Solzhenitsyn regarded himself as a Russian patriot, he has often been assumed to be an imperialist, but the very opposite is true. He regarded Russia's domination of other peoples as a curse. For centuries, the idea that what matters most is imperial power had led Russia into national sin, he affirmed. "All this came to us from Peter I, from the glory of our banners and the so-called 'honor of our Fatherland.' We were crushing our neighbors; we were expanding. And in our Fatherland it became established that: The result is what counts." Bolshevism developed the sinfulness already in us.

Instead of taking pride in the enormous size of the Russian empire, Russians should repent for imprisoning their neighbors, wrote Solzhenitsyn in his essay "Repentance and Self-Limitation." They must acknowledge what they did to the native Siberian peoples. "With regard to all the peoples in and beyond our borders forcibly drawn into our orbit, we can fully purge our guilt by giving them genuine freedom to decide their future for themselves."

It is easy to forget that repentance, to be real, entails "self-limitation." "We are always very ready to limit *others*," Solzhenitsyn cautions, just as we are always ready to excuse ourselves. For a nation as for an individual, "repentance is always difficult. And not only because we must cross the threshold of self-love, but also because our own sins are not so easily visible to us." To see them, we must stop saying: *Look what they did to us!* and say instead: *Look what we did to ourselves!* "We are all guilty, all besmirched. . . . *We, all of us* . . . were the necessary accomplices." Above all, we must stop thinking that evil is committed only by others. We must not imagine that we can eliminate it by destroying the bad people who disagree with us.

Humanity needs to redirect its efforts to the development of the soul. "The turn toward *inward* development, the triumph of inwardness over outwardness, if it ever happens, will be a great turning point in the history of humankind."

Grieving for Peace

Parents Circle–Families Forum brings together bereaved Palestinians and Israelis.

CHRIS ZIMMERMAN

On the fateful morning of October 7, 2023, a surprise attack carried out by Hamas left more than a thousand Israelis dead and some 250 taken hostage, setting off a military counterattack on Gaza that has left it in ruins and claimed an estimated 72,000 Palestinian lives. Ever since then, it has been almost impossible to say anything about the situation in the region without upsetting somebody. But that has not deterred Parents Circle–Families Forum. A nonprofit that brings together bereaved families from both sides of the conflict, PCFF has never stopped speaking

Chris Zimmerman lives at Harlem House, the Bruderhof's community house in New York City.

Robi Damelin (left) and Bushra Awad, members of PCFF from opposite sides who each lost a son to violence.

out and working toward a peaceful future. Indeed, its members argue, such a path is not only possible but the only viable way forward.

Started by Yitzhak Frankenthal, an Israeli Jew, in 1995 after his son Arik, an IDF soldier, was killed by Hamas, PCFF limits membership to Israelis and Palestinians who have lost immediate family members to violence in the region. Since October 2023, at least eighty new families have joined this club no one wanted to be a part of. The group's effectiveness arises from the shared perspectives of fellow sufferers bound by the knowledge that they have all paid the same terrible price.

Today PCFF has more than eight hundred members. Two in particular – an Israeli Jew and a Palestinian Arab who each lost a child – gained international fame after novelist Colum McCann featured their unlikely friendship in his 2020 novel *Apeirogon*.

One of them, Rami Elhanan, was born in Jerusalem to a Holocaust survivor and became an officer in the Israeli army, fighting in the 1973 Yom Kippur War. In 1997, he lost his fourteen-year-old daughter, Smadar, to a Palestinian suicide bomber. He joined PCFF a year later, after Frankenthal invited him to one of the group's regular sessions – a jarring but ultimately disarming experience, as he told me:

> At first, I thought: these crazy people! But this meeting changed my life. I was forty-seven at the time, but I'm ashamed to say that it was the first time I had ever met Palestinians as human beings. I decided to join the group the next day.

The other, Bassam Aramin, was born near Hebron in 1969. At sixteen, he was sent to prison after throwing a hand grenade at an Israeli army jeep (no one was killed or injured). While behind bars, he unexpectedly learned "to see Jews as humans," and following his release, he cofounded Combatants for Peace, an organization made up of former soldiers from both sides of the conflict. In 2007, his ten-year-old daughter, Abir, was hit in the head by a stray rubber bullet fired by Israeli forces. She died three days later. It was after this that – through Elhanan – he got to know PCFF and eventually joined.

NATURALLY, THE EVENTS of October 2023 and its aftermath have affected PCFF, and Elhanan and Aramin personally, in every conceivable way. In Aramin's words: "We cannot travel. We cannot meet physically – everything happens via Zoom. But we will not be silent. Our suffering has given us a certain moral authority and an obligation to keep raising our voices to share the message we believe in."

> **"Our suffering has given us a certain moral authority, and an obligation to keep raising our voices to share the message we believe in."** —Bassam Aramin

Dialogue – its importance and its limitations – was at the heart of a conversation I had about PCFF with Greg Khalil last November. An American-born Palestinian, Khalil is the head of Telos, a US-based nonprofit working for peace in the Middle East region. He is not a member of PCFF, but supports its work:

> One problem many people have with promoting dialogue is that it can lead to normalization. In fact, people often leave such a dialogue more deeply wounded and more entrenched in their positions than before.
>
> In the case of PCFF, however, there's a difference. The sort of dialogue they promote grows out of a shared purpose: a realization that all sides have a common claim – our common humanity – which cannot be ignored or denied. We may never agree

> on this or that solution, but those disagreements are always an expression of deeper core values, and as long as we can hone in on those and find empathy, we will be able to keep talking.
>
> Engaging in such conversations is often deeply uncomfortable – even dangerous – because it can destabilize what we think. It can trigger fears. But that's precisely why it's so important. PCFF takes all these big, complex historical and political questions and distills them, boils them down, to one fundamental argument: that it's not permissible to use the slaughter of your own children to justify the slaughter of other children; or to put it another way, that you cannot use the loss of your own loved ones to excuse the sacrificing of other lives.

Interviewing Aramin and Elhanan by phone, I asked them how they envisioned moving from sharing personal stories to addressing the larger structural problems that lead to war. Could building empathy between individuals really make a difference on an international level? Aramin was emphatic:

> Absolutely. Empathy is everything. If you lose your empathy for others, you lose your humanity. You become a monster. And you can only have empathy for someone if you know what they have suffered – if you are willing to listen to them and talk with them. This has the power to bring change at all levels of society. Of course, dialogue alone is not going to solve the problem. Our goal is for Israelis and Palestinians to enjoy freedom and democracy and peace and security together. But in the meantime, we will keep promoting dialogue.

Ari Goldman, a former writer for the *New York Times* and professor at Columbia Journalism School, taught a religion class there with Greg Khalil for six years. Together, they took students to the Holy Land to give them "the broader perspective gained by hearing as many stories as possible." In early 2025, Goldman hosted members of PCFF at Columbia. Reflecting on the experience, he told me:

> There is such a divide between the narratives, and such a tendency for everyone to remain stuck in their own grief, that there's very little common ground for people to find. PCFF is an example of a group that helps people to reach beyond their own horror and to embrace someone else – another human being who is going through the same or similar thing – on a visceral level.
>
> It's terrible that this is where we are forced to find common ground, and I'm sure that for many people who are suffering, PCFF makes grieving even harder. Many would probably prefer to retreat and build walls than talk to others who have suffered, but that makes those who do participate – those who have found a lesson in all of this – all the more remarkable.

When I asked him to explain what he meant by "lesson," he said, "The lesson is that we're all hurting – and not just one side of the conflict. The lesson is that we're all human beings."

The same clarity of purpose marked a PCFF event I attended in New York City in October 2025. As at every forum hosted by the group, there were speakers from both sides of the conflict. Liora Eilon, a retiree from Kibbutz Kfar Aza, spoke first. A former civics and history teacher, she was caught right in the middle of the October 7 massacre. Seeking shelter in the safe room of her home and hiding there for forty-eight hours, she emerged to learn that her son, the leader of the commune's civilian defense unit, had been killed. So had dozens of other kibbutz members.

Eilon's counterpart at the event was Mohamed Abu Jafar. Born and raised in the West Bank, he was fourteen when, in 2002, he witnessed the death of his sixteen-year-old brother at the hands of Israeli soldiers who shot him and then barred bystanders from coming to his aid. The incident led him to study nursing – to give his life

to "healing others." Now a graduate student in public health at Georgetown, Abu Jafar has served as a facilitator at PCFF's summer youth camps and told us about their work in bringing together young Israelis and Palestinians in Cyprus.

As is the practice at PCFF events, Eilon and Abu Jafar simply shared their stories – that is, they made no attempts to speak as representatives for their sides of the conflict. They also declined to promote any particular solution. Afterward, Eilon fielded a question about her work as a peace educator. She has spoken to thousands of young Israelis since October 2023, many of them on the cusp of joining the Israeli Defense Forces. While not a pacifist – she is unyielding about the necessity for self-defense – she always pleads with prospective soldiers to remember that there are human beings on both sides of every conflict. "Don't lose your own humanity as you defend ours."

As for Abu Jafar, he said that while growing up in Jenin, he had never thought of Israelis as fellow humans but only as oppressors. After his brother's death, however, two Israeli mothers from PCFF reached out to his mother; it was she who dragged him to a meeting where he met a "refusenik" – an IDF soldier who had been jailed for refusing to serve in the occupied territories. The meeting transformed him.

Both Abu Jafar and Eilon noted an apparent difference between American and Israeli audiences they speak to: the Americans tend to gravitate toward abstractions like the future of Jerusalem; their arguments are (understandably) far more likely to be informed by their favorite social media platform or newsfeed.

Robi Damelin, a PCFF member I met last December, noted the same. A South African-born Israeli who moved to the country in 1967, she lost her son David to a Palestinian sniper in 2002. Three months later she joined PCFF. Today she is a spokeswoman on its administrative staff.

> People love to talk about the Middle East even if they have no personal connections there. They

Rami Elhanan (left) and Bassam Aramin, members of PCFF, hold photographs of their daughters, Smadar Elhanan (right) and Abir Aramin.

throw around loaded terms like "colonialism" and "genocide." But how many of them can name even one dead person? Who are they helping?

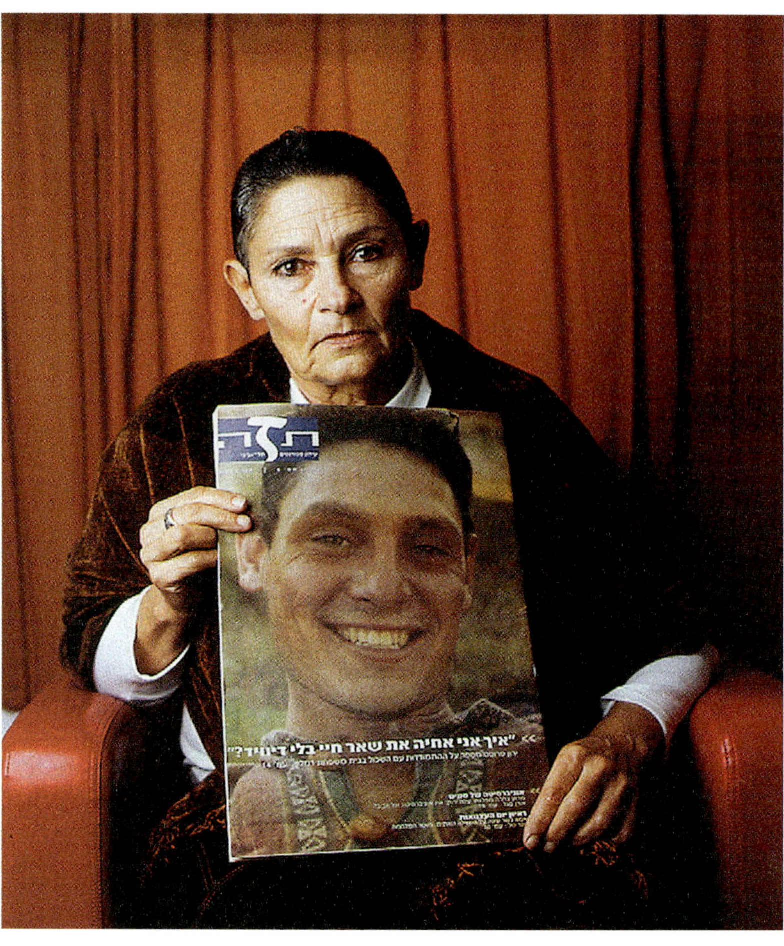

Damelin concedes that there is a place for protest – "of course people have a right to speak up in public on anything they feel deeply about" – yet questions its merits:

> Sure, you can try to draw attention to something by joining a demonstration, but at a certain point I wonder if it doesn't become self-serving. It's nice to have a cause you can serve without compromise when you live in safety – in New Jersey or New York, for instance. But who does it help? And a lot of what goes on in the name of protest these days is so fractured, one wonders what it can possibly achieve. People don't really even coexist anymore: they are totally isolated, living in a million parallel universes, obsessed with their own personal information channels.
>
> If you want to do something constructive, why not find an organization working to end the conflict and start supporting it – even morally, if you don't have the money to do more. There are so many that could use support: Breaking the Silence, Women Wage Peace, Combatants for Peace. Why not find one whose aims speak to you? Join hands with others. Maybe *that* could make a difference.

Asked about her own journey from bereaved mother to international peace activist, she answered by relating the event that changed her from someone who, in her own words, was good at "talking the talk" to someone who was willing to "walk the walk."

> One night three soldiers came to my door to tell me they had caught the sniper who killed David. After that – with that information – what was I to do? There was no person, no face before. No one to forgive. I had been pleased with myself for traveling the world and talking about peace. But did I mean it? Eventually I wrote to the parents of the sniper and told them about David. I told them that we should meet – that we owed this to our children

Robi Damelin holds a photograph of her son, David.

> and grandchildren. I also called for the release of the sniper, more than once, if it would bring about the release of an Israeli hostage.

I asked her how she could be so generous – whether she wasn't tempted by dreams of revenge. She shook her head vigorously:

> How would that have helped? The search for revenge eventually destroys your capacity to achieve anything. It doesn't bring your child back. You have a choice, you know. You can move forward in your life by remembering the loved one you lost in a positive way: by building a monument or establishing a scholarship, or something like that. Or you can become embittered and slowly die. Whereas talking with others brings about the emotional breakthrough that enables trust. When you discover shared pain, you discover a common basis for change.

Like Eilon, Damelin has traveled up and down Israel since October 2023. In the south, where the massacre took place, she took in "the smell of death, rusting tricycles, burned-out houses." She knows there are countless similar scenes in Gaza. Still, she has hope. I asked her why. "Why do I have hope?" she asked in return. "How could I be cynical? If I didn't have hope, I would just sit at home, useless to myself and everyone else. I can't afford to give up. I have grandchildren. Their future is important to me."

I asked Damelin about the PCFF's Youth Ambassador program and the international summer peace camps it runs. After the camps, the Israeli and Palestinian participants return to very different realities. Could this compromise the fruitfulness of dialogue? Damelin demurred. Whatever disparities there are, she said, and whatever criticism might arise because of them make PCFF's peace programs even more vital, if only because they "help young people put themselves in the shoes of the other." She added that no matter how imperfect, dialogue is the one thing that can yield the "common ground of shared humanity and shared suffering" that brings about peace. "And the younger that starts, the better."

Bassam Aramin would concur. Quoting Martin Luther King Jr., he said, "In the end, we will not remember the words of our enemies, but the silence of our friends." He went on, "We are not asking you to take sides; we are simply asking you not to keep silent. It doesn't matter who is suffering. Keep raising your voice for peace, because none of us lives alone in this world. We are all connected to one another."

"Talking brings about the emotional breakthrough that enables trust. When you discover shared pain, you discover a common basis for change." —Robi Damelin

As for Damelin's refusal to yield to cynicism, and her stubborn hope, Rami Elhanan shares both:

> If you look back in history, people would never have dreamed that the British and the French and the Germans would become partners. We never thought the Berlin Wall would come down. We never thought that apartheid would end in South Africa or that there could be peace in Northern Ireland. But all these things have happened.

In the meantime, Abu Jafar and Eilon make no bones about it: being a "peacenik" these days is not likely to evoke admiration. On the contrary, plenty of people think they're crazy. Eilon shrugs. "Call me what you want," she says. "I know who I am and what I'm working for."

SCANDIA
EST OMNIS DIVISA IN PARTES TRES
QUARVM VNAM INCOLVNT lappi
ALIAM lappalaiset, TERTIAM, QUI
IPSORVM LINGUA sábmi, NOSTRA finnoi APELLANTVR.
DE Bello Scandico
HVCVSQVE EXTENDITVR REGNVM SVECIE
GERMANIA
Sámeæna lœ
jukkujuvvun njalljie,
ii gålma oassái. Vuostasis
årrut lappar, nubbis
lappalaiset, goalmat
ЛОПАРЕЙ, ja
njalljåt oasis fas
sábmelaččat,
dårugillii
gåččuduvvun
finner,
dahje
sk(r)itfinnar.
BIARMIA
MOSCOVIE PARS
LATHVIA
LITHAVIA
MARE BALTICUM
EST-LANDIA
MARE SVETICUM
SINVS FINONICVM
SVECIA
FINLANDIA
MARE BOT NI CVM
LAPPLANDIA
CARELIA
LAPPIA
SCRITOBINI
CAAMOB
DANIA REGNVM
GOHTENBURG
VERMELANDIA
OSLO
BERGEN
AKERSHVS
TILEMARCHIA
NORVEGIÆ PARS
DOWREFIELD
WALDRES
MOERE
TRONDEM
IEMPHIA
FINMARCHIA
UPMEJE
SKIELLET
LULEJU
BITUN

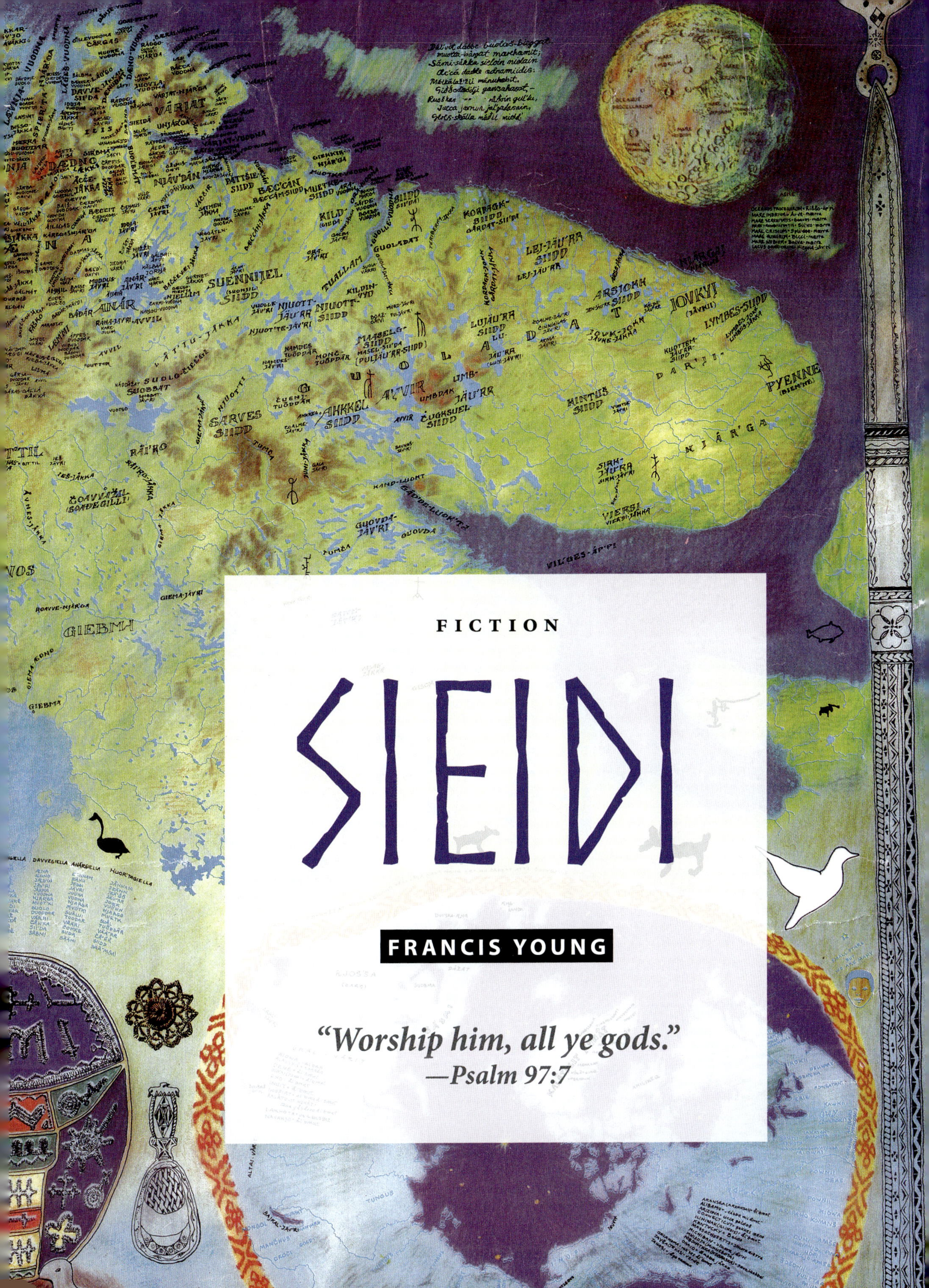

FICTION

SIEIDI

FRANCIS YOUNG

"Worship him, all ye gods."
—Psalm 97:7

IN ALL THE YEARS SINCE, I'VE NEVER REGRETTED WHAT WE DID.

NO ONE WAS TALKING about restitution of artifacts in those days – I don't think anyone would even have thought about it, not among curators anyway. It wasn't something I thought about either – I can't claim to have been ahead of my time, because I didn't do it of my own accord. I needed a good deal of prompting, and that prompting just came in a particularly strange form. It all began the day I first caught sight of the *sieidi*, although if I'm honest I had no idea what it was. I had just started working at the National Museum a few weeks earlier, and I was still mostly confined to the basement and the storage areas – the senior curators wouldn't let me near the actual exhibitions yet.

It was when I was moving some boxes that I caught sight of it, covered in thick gray dust under an air vent. It wasn't large – about two feet tall – and my first thought was that it was just some old lumber. But it was too peculiar-looking for that. Yes, it was made of wood – but there was a degree of deliberation in its haphazard construction, with smaller sticks carefully lodged in knotholes in the main trunk, which terminated in a flurry of twigs that looked a little like a head of hair. Indeed, the way the bole expanded at the top of the trunk and the sticks shot out from its sides gave it an almost anthropomorphic appearance. Almost, but not quite.

I had seen crude figurines before, and it usually

Opening spread: The Sábmi map (1975) by Hans Ragnar Mathisen is a work of indigenous cartography that seeks to reclaim the geography of the Sámi people.

wasn't hard to sense even an ambiguous depiction of the human form – after all, even very young children can manage to create that. Whatever this was, it wasn't unskillful; great care had been taken to construct it, yet for some reason it only hinted at the human form – as if pointing to something else. Out of curiosity I moved the boxes a little further. There was a sort of parcel-tag hanging from one of the sticks (we used to put those on some of the larger artifacts in storage) and on it there was just one word: "SIEIDI." Fortunately there was also an accession number on the back. I recognized *sieidi* as a Sámi word – not that I knew anything then about Sámi languages, but I had been involved in cataloguing a few Sámi artifacts and it had come up, although I couldn't remember what it meant. At any rate, I found a pencil in my pocket and scribbled down the accession number before I pushed the boxes back into position.

I was eager to get away from work that afternoon because I had agreed to meet Ella in a café on Karl Johans gate; we had been seeing one another for about three months at that point, and Ella was working for Norwegian Church Aid. I hadn't met her parents yet, but she had mentioned she had some Sámi heritage – I couldn't remember whether from a grandparent or great-grandparent, but she knew a little bit about Sámi things. That was more than could be said of most Norwegians in those days – it was before the Alta Dam protests were on our television screens, or anything like that.

I wondered if Ella knew what *sieidi* meant, so when we were settled in the café I asked her.

"I think I came across a Sámi word today," I said.

"Oh?" She leaned forward with interest, her long dark hair framing her smiling face as she clutched a cup of herbal tea.

"Yes. S-I-E-I-D-I." I was worried about mis-pronouncing it, so I spelled it out letter by letter.

Francis Young is a historian, folklorist, indexer, and translator based in the United Kingdom. His most recent book, Silence of the Gods, *was published by Cambridge University Press in June 2025.*

A *sieidi* in Eastern Lapland.

Ella laughed. "*Sieidi.* It's a holy thing in Sámi culture. Like a rock or something. A special place in the landscape."

"Was it your grandmother you said was Sámi?"

"My great-grandmother," she corrected me. "Honestly, I really don't know much about Sámi culture. I wish I knew more."

"Have you ever been – I mean, to Finnmark?"

She shook her head. "No. I've never been farther north than Trondheim."

The conversation passed on to other things. I decided not to mention the strange object I had found behind the boxes. I was confused by what Ella had said about rocks and landscapes. Whatever it was, the thing was clearly not a rock.

However, I had the accession number in my pocket and so, the next day, I consulted the card indexes and found the original catalogue entry for the *sieidi*:

> Lapp *sieidi*. Wood. Age unknown. From Sálajok, Finnmark. The crudely anthropomorphic figurine was recovered close to a lake from a site of sacrifice by Nils Olavsen in 1921.

It was a tiny amount of information, but it raised many questions. Clearly, it was possible for a *sieidi* to be something other than a rock. But where was Sálajok? And what did the catalogue mean by "a site of sacrifice"? What was the *sieidi* still doing there in 1921, and in what sense was it "recovered"? And who was Nils Olavsen?

This final question was probably the easiest to answer. I had no time to look further that day, but when I had a moment from my duties the following day, I made my way to the small archaeological library inside the National Museum – it smelled of mingled pipe-smoke, yellowing paper, and peeling adhesive tape – and looked up Olavsen in the card index there. After all, if he had been collecting artifacts for the National Museum in the twenties he was probably an archaeologist, and probably wrote something. Sure enough, there was a card for Nils Olavsen with a couple of entries on it: *The Earliest Churches of Finnmark* (1920) and *The Mission of Erasmus Wallund* (1922). Given his interest in churches and missions, I wondered if Olavsen (in common with many investigators of Lapland) had been a missionary as well as an antiquarian – and sure enough, when I tracked down the second of his monographs he was pictured in a black-and-white plate, in the ruff of a clergyman, incongruously combined with a then-fashionable thin moustache and stiffly slicked hair.

There was nothing in either of these books about the *sieidi* downstairs, but turning to the conclusion of *The Mission of Erasmus Wallund,* I found a passage that perhaps gave some insight into Olavsen's religious views:

> The old idolatry that Wallund strove against is very nearly dead among the Lapps, although in a few places a *passe-warck* is still to be found in some remote place where fresh carcasses of reindeer are offered to the *sieidi*. Yet the active efforts of the clergy and magistrates in removing those *sieidis* that can be displaced, such as smaller stones and idols of wood, have greatly reduced the number of such sites of sacrifice while endowing the nation's museums and centers of learning with valuable artifacts testifying to the unique religion of the Lapps.

The book continued in this vein, combining a genuine curiosity about Sámi culture on Olavsen's part with an equally certain belief that its religious and spiritual aspects, at least, were best eradicated and replaced by the light of modern education.

But if the clergyman's intent had been to bring the *sieidi* to Oslo for scholars to study it, then it was something of an indictment of his project that the thing was now sitting, forgotten and covered in dust, in the basement of the National Museum fifty years later. The thought made me rather sad; as surely as the hammer of an iconoclast, the cold cataloging hand of the curator robs an artifact of its sacredness.

That night I struggled to get to sleep as the *sieidi*, a mute witness to a vanished way of life in Finnmark, loomed in my imagination. Between sleep and waking, I imagined dark lakes between snow-covered hills, peculiar rocks and dead trees, mysterious clefts where Sámi in bright-colored clothing butchered reindeer in the hope of success in hunting or fishing. What had we done by taking this thing from another world, and what purpose was served by keeping it where no one would see it – at least, not unless a senior curator decided to dust it off and incorporate it into an exhibition on the Sámi? And that, I reflected, might never happen.

I HAD BEEN UNSURE whether to tell Ella about the *sieidi*, and in the end it was not so much her passing interest in Sámi things that led me to do so, but rather my own selfish desire to unburden myself of a thought that was troubling me. When I had finished laying out the entire story and my thoughts about the *sieidi* – we were in a little German restaurant in Gamle Oslo, almost deserted – Ella was silent for a while.

"Yes, there are some *sieidis* that are like that. Bits of tree and wood. They were the easiest to take away."

"It seems wrong, somehow, that it was just removed like that. Do you think it was still a site of sacrifice, even as late as the twenties?" I asked her.

She shook her head. "I don't know. I have heard stories about sacrifices carrying on really late, right up to the War."

That was all Ella said about it then, although she seemed a little subdued for the rest of the evening. She was like that sometimes; it took her a while to process something difficult, so I didn't push her on it. We stayed late, and it was getting dark by the time I walked Ella back to the apartment she shared with three other girls. It was in Gamle Oslo too, so it wasn't far – in one of those old-fashioned blocks, four stories high and painted yellow. In the light of the street lamps, the yellow seemed even more intense. As we reached the block I glanced up and saw a reassuring light on in her apartment.

I was wishing Ella goodnight, and about to kiss her on the cheek, when she suddenly pulled away from me. She pointed silently to the end of the street. It had been empty when we turned into it – it wasn't very long, in fact – but now as I turned back to look in the direction Ella was pointing I saw the unbelievable sight: it was, of all things, a reindeer. The creature was just standing there, its head raised up and looking straight at us, a splendid pair of antlers spread above its head; the streetlamps gave it an almost unearthly halo, and the color of its coat was pure white. I was surprised we hadn't

Small rocks placed on the Áhkku *sieidi* rock formation near Alta, Norway.

heard it – the streets here were still mostly cobbled, but the animal was completely silent.

I turned back to Ella; I was smiling at the incongruity of the sight, thinking about how my parents wouldn't believe me when I told them I'd seen a reindeer on the streets of Oslo. But Ella wasn't smiling. Her face was as white as the reindeer. When I glanced back, the reindeer was gone, as suddenly as it had come. Ella looked at me – the sight had clearly troubled her deeply – and she muttered one word before she turned to enter her building: "Miyandash."

I DIDN'T KNOW WHAT IT MEANT, of course. In the end, I didn't mention the reindeer to my mother and father; it felt like something that should stay between Ella and me. I supposed there must be a rational explanation for a reindeer wandering Oslo – I'd seen people in Sámi costumes lead them around at Christmastime to be petted by children. But it seemed so much stranger to see an unaccompanied reindeer wandering the streets of the capital in summer. Clearly it had escaped from somewhere. But there was one detail about the reindeer that seemed especially peculiar, and that was its whiteness. The streetlamps lent everything a yellowish hue, and although one of them had been shining directly onto the reindeer, it had remained a bright white. An optical illusion of some kind, I reflected.

Still, Ella had seemed troubled enough that I rode the tram to Gamle Oslo early the next morning – I didn't care if I was late for work – and tried to catch her before she left. As it turned out, she was still at home; her housemate Kari let me in, and I found Ella sitting on her bed, gazing toward the window, holding a cup of coffee. She smiled weakly as I came in; I cleared some of the books and clothes off a chair and perched on it.

"That word you said last night," I said. "That's another Sámi thing, isn't it?"

She lowered her eyes. "It's one of the stories my half-Sámi grandmother told me – she got it from her mother. Miyandash is the holy white reindeer. He's supposed to be the ancestor of the Sámi people – sometimes a man, sometimes a reindeer, sometimes a sort of hybrid reindeer-man."

"You think the reindeer was supernatural?"

She shook her head. "Honestly, I don't know. I don't know if Miyandash is real. I don't know if that was him. But I do believe in signs. I don't think something that strange would happen without a reason. And you saw how that reindeer was still white, even under the streetlamps?"

I nodded. "I noticed that, yes."

"You know there's nothing more important to the Sámi than reindeer. First you come across that *sieidi*, then you tell me about it, then we see an impossible reindeer." She lifted her eyes to meet mine. "It's a message, and it's about the *sieidi*."

And then she said it.

"We need to put it back."

I almost laughed, but I checked myself. "Put it back? Are you serious, Ella? Put it back where?"

"By that lake in Sálajok."

"Which is where, exactly?"

She turned away, clearly disappointed. "Why do you have to be so cynical? I want to be alone. Please go."

I left as she asked, but I felt awful. I knew, deep down, that this could be the breaking point of our relationship, that if Ella and I couldn't agree on this issue, we would get no further as a couple. And I didn't want that to happen. Like so many young men, I hadn't yet said it to her because I hadn't yet realized it, but I loved Ella. There was no getting past that. I had to go along with this, because this – however mad it seemed – was the next step.

I rang her that evening.

"We need to talk about how to put the *sieidi* back."

STEALING A FORGOTTEN ARTIFACT from storage in the National Museum, if you were a junior curator, wasn't especially difficult in

those days. I had a plan for that. But there were a lot of other things we needed plans for that I had never thought about. Most importantly, we had to find Sálajok on a map. Luckily, there were plenty of these in the National Museum, and I began using all my breaks to pull out and search through endlessly detailed topographical maps of Finnmark. At long last, somewhere between Tromsø and Kautokeino, I came across a Sálajok that was in the vicinity of a lake. I placed tracing paper over that section of the map and carefully copied the entire section in pencil, then marked the area on a copy of a larger-scale map of Finnmark to remove any doubt about the location. Of course, that didn't mean we knew where the "site of sacrifice" was located – we just had to find the general area of Sálajok and hope we somehow stumbled across it.

And then there was the journey. Neither of us owned a car, and the drive to Sálajok was two thousand kilometers. I knew my father would never let me borrow his car, but in the end Ella reached an agreement with her housemate Kari, a junior doctor who didn't usually need her car for work. Borrowing the car forced us to choose a date for our departure; and so, at the beginning of June, our plan went into action. We both asked for a week's leave (and got it, surprisingly enough), and I found a military surplus rucksack that was large enough to comfortably accommodate the *sieidi*.

The plan for stealing the *sieidi* was straightforward enough. One of the senior curators had been asking me, for some time, to bring some boxes of old engravings upstairs for cataloging. As he wasn't my boss, I hadn't done a great deal about it, but on the day before my leave was due to begin I suddenly took on the task enthusiastically. Finding one of the boxes that contained various long engraved panoramas of old Oslo and other cities, I removed a few of them in order to make a space large enough for the *sieidi,* and simply carried it upstairs in the box. When I saw that the coast was clear, I took the box into the staff locker room and, in a heart-stopping minute, transferred the *sieidi* from the box to my rucksack, hoping no one would walk through the door. I then calmly took the box upstairs, followed by the rest of the boxes, and at the end of the day, took the rucksack with its unusual contents to Ella's flat.

"So – are you ready?"

Ella placed the rucksack carefully in a corner of her bedroom.

"You don't want to see it?" I asked.

She shook her head. "I still feel bad about taking it. We are stealing from the National Museum, after all. It's just that I'd feel worse about not trying to put it back."

"Well," I said, "I don't think anyone will miss it. Not for a while, at least. I made sure I removed it from the card index as well, so the only record will be if it's in a printed catalog somewhere, or a book. But it's not exactly unusual for an artifact mentioned in an old book to be nowhere to be seen in the museum's collections. I think it will take years – decades, maybe – for anyone to realize it's been taken."

"I hope you're right. For your sake."

And then she told me how grateful she was to me; I blushed embarrassedly, made my excuses, and left.

It was Friday evening; our plan was not to leave immediately the next day, but to set off in the early hours of the morning on Sunday, when no one would see us driving off. So it was that we loaded the rucksack with the *sieidi* into Kari's orange Kadett very early on Sunday morning, before dawn, and drove to Trondheim. It was a punishing initiation to long-distance driving, for me at least, but after around six hours, we entered the medieval city in the middle of the morning. The bells of Nidaros Cathedral were peeling out for the morning service. Ella had slept for most of the journey; she now said she wanted to go to the service. I wasn't a believer then, so it didn't interest me; I loitered in the square outside the great west front of the cathedral, listening to the faint sound of the organ permeating the air around me.

When Ella came out of the cathedral she was smiling.

"You seem happier!" I remarked.

"I prayed about the *sieidi*, and God told me I'm doing the right thing."

I knew Ella had felt conflicted about stealing the artifact, and implicating me in the theft.

She continued, "I don't think what was stolen to begin with can be stolen, if you just want to put it back. And I think the *sieidi* wants to go back too."

I laughed. "God must approve of pagan idols, if he wants the *sieidi* back at the site of sacrifice. Maybe you need to decide if you're a Lutheran or a Sámi pagan, Ella!"

She shook her head. "I don't think it's like that. A *sieidi* isn't an idol. That's what the missionaries called them, but they're something else."

Whether God or Miyandash was on our side, or perhaps both, I reflected that we needed all the help we could get if we were going to drive the whole length of Norway. It was Ella's turn to get us to Mosjøen by nightfall – not that there would be much of a nightfall as we drew ever closer to the land of the midnight sun. We got to the little town, surrounded by densely wooded hills, at around seven o'clock. Ella found a place to park that was secluded enough for us to avoid notice. She had brought drapes to hang over the car windows, although they didn't do much to block out the sunlight that still lit the sky throughout the night. She curled up on the back seat while I did my best to get to sleep in the tipped-back passenger seat. I drifted off for a short while, but when I woke at four o'clock in the morning, I found it impossible to get back to sleep. I tore off the drape from the windscreen, shifted into the driver's seat, and began the next leg of the journey (to Narvik) while Ella was still asleep.

It was midday on Monday by the time we reached Narvik, and we were in Tromsø by that evening. We knew another night in the car would leave us too exhausted to drive, so we found a hostel in Tromsø. Even the shared dormitories of a student hostel made a welcome change from a car seat – at least there were blinds to exclude the relentless sun, which now hovered all night on the horizon and refused to set. The hardest part of the journey still lay ahead: the long drive around the fjords of northernmost Finnmark was the only way to avoid crossing the border into Finland to reach Kautokeino.

Reindeer skull and other objects deposited in the crevice of the Fállegeađgi *sieidi* stone, Alta, Norway.

A DAY OR SO LATER, Ella and I were struggling up a low but deceptively exhausting rise – almost entirely treeless but for an occasional stunted mountain birch. The hillside was a sea of ground-hugging mountain crowberry and florid matgrass, interspersed with flowers blooming hurriedly in the frenzied

subarctic summer that was always over almost as soon as it had begun. But here we were in the midst of it, I with the *sieidi* in a rucksack on my back as we trudged up and down in search of the lake of Sálajok. I had no illusions that Sálajok would be an actual *place* as I might have understood it – a village or a settlement. We had little chance of running into any permanent human habitation here, and we had nothing to navigate by but the traced copies of maps I had made in the National Museum and a compass embedded in a walking stick that once belonged to Ella's grandfather. Our trudge to the top of this latest rise was another attempt to get high enough to catch sight of the lake of Sálajok, which was the only geographical clue we had for locating the "site of sacrifice." I had lost track of the time – I remained unsure if it was even day or night, as the stubborn sun bathed the low hills in the same golden arctic light regardless of the hour. All I knew was that I was tired, and the rucksack with the *sieidi* was growing heavier all the time.

"I know we'll see it from the top here – I know it!" Ella assured me as she strode ahead, walking stick in hand.

But the slope seemed interminable – one of those hills whose gradient is so gentle (yet so punishing over time) that you never seem to reach the summit. I felt I could go no further – this was a fool's errand. Of course I had been an idiot to think that I could find one place in a trackless country of proverbial vastness with nothing more than a name on a map. I had begun to think through how I was going to break it to Ella that the task was hopeless – how to talk her down from her seeming blind faith that the spot could be found. And at the back of my mind, always, was the question of whether I had done enough; was *trying* to return the *sieidi* enough to fulfill what I owed her? Or would she never forgive me for our collective failure to achieve our aim?

I had just summoned the courage to speak when Ella preempted me with a wild yell.

"There! There!" She was gesticulating toward

what I took to be the top of the rise, though it was farther off to our right than I had expected.

"What is it?"

"Can't you see it?"

And then I did see it – a glimpse of antlers, brilliant white, just above the line of the horizon – before the reindeer stepped into view. Ella was weeping with joy.

"I knew he'd lead us there!"

It was certainly a remarkable sight. I knew reindeer were herd animals, so to encounter a buck on his own like this was already rather unusual – even if I could set aside the remarkable coincidence of his brilliant white color. Perhaps Ella was right. But right or wrong, she had broken into a run for the spot where the reindeer stood, and I could barely keep up with her. When I next looked up there was no reindeer, but Ella's course was true, and within a few minutes we stood in the right place. It was as if the entire landscape had opened up, like a showman lifting the shutter on a peepshow, and we saw a black lake beneath us in a cleft between two wooded hills that we would never have found without reaching this position.

Ella was dancing on the hilltop. And then she pulled me close to her, and she kissed me – for the first time since Oslo – and it was as if her exhilaration passed to me in that kiss. I danced too, and whooped and yelled, exhausted as I was. Here was the lake of Sálajok!

GETTING TO THE LAKE WASN'T EASY – between us and the water lay a labyrinth of dark rocks almost bereft of soil, stained with white and yellow lichen. But we knew where we were going now, and I felt as though I had passed beyond unbelief into a baffling new world of trust where I *knew* the reindeer would guide us to the place of the *sieidi*. There was no way to articulate it rationally; as far as I was concerned, the facts had not changed, but for the first time in my life I was living by faith. A wholly new factor was present in my sense of self.

At long last, somehow, we scrambled down rock scree onto the pebbles of the lakeshore. The white reindeer was waiting for us there. He trotted ahead – a long way ahead, it seemed – and we simply followed. The place of sacrifice was where two faces of rock came together – almost like a kiss – leaving a deep cleft sunk into the ground above, and an arch-like aperture below. The reindeer stopped there, then was gone.

I suspected that the place of sacrifice was not the cave-like space below – which seemed empty – but somewhere above us; and sure enough, there were natural steps of a kind leading upward that invited our ascent. Ella reached the top first, and I found her gazing down at the bleached reindeer skulls – ancient now, probably – that still rested in the cleft from the last sacrifices made generations ago, in honor of the *sieidi*: in honor of the singularity and strangeness of this one place on God's earth. I understood now that the *sieidi* was not that place, nor was it the idol that the missionaries thought it was. It was, rather, a waymarker – a sort of bookmark that held this place for anyone who sought it.

It was as I gazed along the bone-strewn sacrificial gash in the rock that I first caught sight of a bright white cross placed in the space where the two faces of rock almost met, as if to join them. Had the cross been placed there by Nils Olavsen, when he removed the *sieidi*? It hardly looked half a century old if so, and gleamed as if newly painted. In that moment it scarcely mattered; the time had come to return the *sieidi*; to put the bookmark back between the right pages. I knelt down, undid the rucksack, and, cradling the strange wooden burden, stepped carefully into the cleft as far as I could safely go. By now I had learned to trust that the *sieidi* would find its own place. Glancing back at Ella, and then at the bright white cross, I let the *sieidi* go.

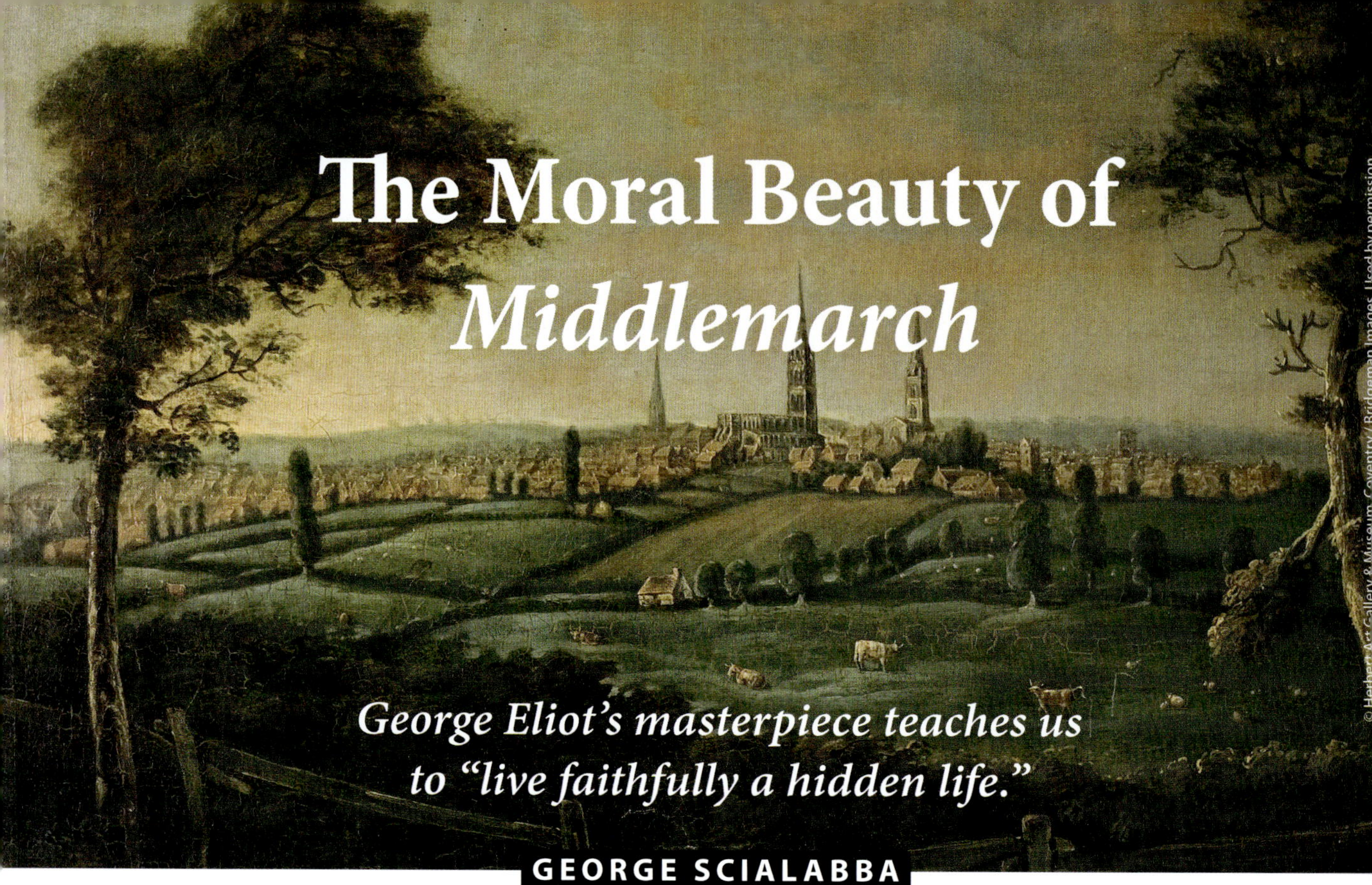

The Moral Beauty of *Middlemarch*

George Eliot's masterpiece teaches us to "live faithfully a hidden life."

GEORGE SCIALABBA

"Worship the Lord in the beauty of holiness," says the psalmist (29:2). Many spiritual writers have discoursed on this theme, including, curiously, Jonathan Edwards, better known for terrifying congregations with his famous 1741 sermon on "Sinners in the Hands of an Angry God." "The moral beauty of God… nothing can withstand," he writes in his *Religious Affections* (1746). "All the spiritual beauty of [Christ's] human nature, consisting in his meekness, lowliness, patience, heavenliness, love to God, love to men, condescension to the mean and vile, and compassion to the miserable, etc. all is summed up in his holiness."

"Moral beauty" is an arresting phrase. Typically, goodness is commended for its effects rather than for its aspect. Perhaps the scarcity nowadays of such lofty sacred eloquence as Edwards's, the drabness of much preaching and religious writing compared with earlier periods, when sermons were literary performances and widely published, is part of the general verbal aridity of our age, brought on by the ubiquitous toxic blooms of commercial speech that convert our innermost thoughts into advertising jingles. This is by no means only a loss for believers; the religious imagination is a vital part of a living culture. Ceding it – like so much of contemporary culture – to formula and cliché gradually but inexorably hollows us out.

There are, no doubt, plenty of resources within Christian and other religious traditions from which to relearn heartfelt eloquence. But I'd like to propose a secular exemplar: perhaps the greatest repository of moral beauty in English literature, the voice of the narrator in George Eliot's *Middlemarch*.

George Eliot (1819–1880) was born Marian Evans to an estate manager and his wife in Warwickshire. She was extremely plain, and

Coventry from the East, oil on canvas, ca. 1830. Artist unknown.

Perhaps the greatest repository of moral beauty in English literature is the voice of the narrator in George Eliot's *Middlemarch*.

though this was in some ways unfortunate for her, it was fortunate for posterity: her family considered her unmarriageable, so she received more of an education than most girls at the time. Though painfully rebuffed by her first crush, the then-famous (now largely forgotten) social theorist Herbert Spencer, she eventually found an ideal partner, the writer and editor George Lewes, who worshipped her. Her formal education was patchy, but her intellectual appetites were voracious. When she began as a literary freelancer – writing under a masculine name – she was brilliantly successful. Though a nonbeliever, she was always keenly interested in and sympathetic toward religion, and early in her career translated into English two of the most influential Christian books of the nineteenth century: *The Life of Jesus* by David Friedrich Strauss and *The Essence of Christianity* by Ludwig Feuerbach. In her late thirties, she began writing novels, producing several masterpieces: *Adam Bede*, *The Mill on the Floss*, *Felix Holt*, *Middlemarch*, and *Daniel Deronda*.

Virginia Woolf called *Middlemarch* "one of the few English novels written for grown-up people." That may have been, as much as anything, a dig at enormously popular novelists like Walter Scott, Charles Dickens, and H. G. Wells; after all, Jane Austen's, Thomas Hardy's, and D. H. Lawrence's novels are arguably grown-up fare. *Middlemarch,* though, is a book to grow up with: an ideal moral education for a college student (as in my case, and that of thousands of others) or young adult. Eliot's running commentary explains, admonishes, predicts, praises, rebukes, and excuses with a wit so gentle and a charity so unfailing that her voice might be said to float like a butterfly and rouse her readers not with a sting but with a light, affectionate nudge.

The central character in *Middlemarch* is Dorothea Brooke, ardent and idealistic – though the book's preface introduces us to another youthful idealist, Saint Teresa of Ávila, who set off as a toddler with her even younger brother to convert the Moors. It is a charming story and gives rise to a reflection that will haunt the rest of the book:

> Many Theresas have been born who found for themselves no epic life wherein there was a constant unfolding of far-resonant action; perhaps only a life of mistakes, the offspring of a certain spiritual

George Scialabba is a book critic and retired building manager at Harvard University. His reviews have appeared in the Boston Globe, Dissent, *the* Nation, *and many other publications. His latest collection,* The Sealed Envelope, *was published by Yale University Press in January 2026.*

John Mayall, *George Eliot,* photographic portrait (albumen print), 1858.

> grandeur ill-matched with the meanness of opportunity; perhaps a tragic failure which found no sacred poet and sank unwept into oblivion.

The innumerable ways that ideals – especially women's – can be defeated by circumstance is one of the novel's most poignant reflections.

In the early nineteenth century, marriage was a foregone conclusion for a rich and beautiful young woman. But instead of accepting the obvious suitor, the rich and handsome owner of the neighboring estate, the unworldly Dorothea decides it is her vocation to marry an elderly clergyman engaged in recondite historico-theological scholarship and to become his helpmeet. Her gradual discovery of his refined selfishness and intellectual sterility is cruelly disappointing. But Edward Casaubon is not a monster nor even an especially bad man. He is merely "the center of his own world" and "liable to think that others were providentially made for him," a trait that is "not quite alien to us and, like the other mendicant hopes of mortals, claims some of our pity." This is Eliot's characteristic tone of reproof: gentle, wry, compassionate, and always insistent that every fault of every character almost certainly has its analog in every reader.

Eliot's characteristic tone of reproof: gentle, wry, compassionate, and always insistent that every fault of every character almost certainly has its analog in every reader.

Mr. Casaubon has a younger, rather romantic cousin, Will Ladislaw, who is as free-spirited and open-hearted as Casaubon is fearful and insecure. Will's mere presence in the fictional town of Middlemarch and his eager but innocent friendship with Dorothea become intolerable to her husband, whose pettiness and suspiciousness poison the already strained marriage. Eliot's judgment of this profoundly unhappy man is a mix of severity and mercy:

> It is an uneasy lot at best, to be what we call highly taught and yet not to enjoy: to be present at this great spectacle of life and never to be liberated from a small hungry shivering self – never to be fully possessed by the glory we behold, never to have our consciousness rapturously transformed into the vividness of a thought, the ardor of a passion, the energy of an action, but always to be scholarly and uninspired, ambitious and timid, scrupulous and dim-sighted.

That every villain is also a victim, to be pitied as well as blamed – *Middlemarch* illustrates this Christian commonplace with consummate literary skill.

Chief among the novel's vast tableau of supporting characters are another pair, Tertius

William Henry Brooke, *Bablake Hospital Coventry,* watercolor, 1819.

Lydgate and Rosamond Vincy. He is a young physician, new to Middlemarch, intellectually ambitious, and determined to remain free (unmarried) until he has made his mark. She is as beautiful as a nymph but small-minded and self-willed, determined to marry above her station – that is, someone with aristocratic connections, like Lydgate. Selfishness is the cardinal sin in *Middlemarch*, and Rosamond is the novel's primary case study, even more than Casaubon.

"Sin" is perhaps too strong: selfishness, for Eliot, is above all a matter of occluded vision, an inability to see things from anyone else's point of view. And that inability, too, may be conditioned by circumstance. Lydgate's is a comparatively innocent selfishness: he needs very little from other people, and his training and gifts allow him to make his own way. But for Rosamond, there appears to be only one way to rise in the world – to captivate and manipulate. Long before meeting Lydgate, she has honed those skills on her pliable parents. In response to her mother's plea to be sensible about expenses, "Rosamond, examining some muslin-work, listened in silence, and at the end gave a certain turn of her graceful neck, of which only long experience could teach you that it meant perfect obstinacy." Her father fared no better:

> Mr. Vincy, blustering as he was, had as little of his own way as if he had been a prime minister: the force of circumstances was easily too much for him, as it is for most pleasure-loving florid men; and the circumstance called Rosamond was particularly forcible by means of that mild persistence which, as we know, enables a white soft living substance to make its way in spite of opposing rock.

Rosamond is a master at putting other people in the wrong – a poisoned gift, which overcomes Lydgate's prudent resolution to wait before marrying. The resulting marriage is disastrous. To satisfy Rosamond's expensive tastes, Lydgate reluctantly puts aside his research and becomes a physician to the rich – a defeated man.

> Rosamond continued to be mild in her temper, inflexible in her judgment, disposed to admonish her husband, and able to frustrate him by stratagem. As the years went on he opposed her less and less, whence Rosamond concluded that he had learned the value of her opinion.... To the last he occasionally let slip a bitter speech which was more memorable than the signs he made of his repentance. He once called her his basil plant; and when she asked for an explanation, said that basil was a plant which had flourished wonderfully on a murdered man's brains.

Rosamond is a chilling object lesson in the futility of getting one's own way at all costs. Dorothea illustrates the opposite lesson: that self-forgetfulness is the royal road, if not to happiness, at least to the depth of feeling that makes life real.

There is one perfectly virtuous resident of Middlemarch: the carpenter, builder, and land agent Caleb Garth. Caleb's entire ambition is to

William Powell Frith, *The Lovers,* oil on board, 1855.

do good work. For the chance to take on "a bit o' needful work," he is apt to forget about negotiating the best possible fee – or any fee – a fault which his long-suffering wife both deplores and smiles at. With touches of religious language, Eliot portrays Garth as a secular saint:

> I think his virtual divinities were good practical schemes, accurate work, and the faithful completion of undertakings: his prince of darkness was a slack workman . . . he was ready to accept any number of [beliefs about the universe] if they did not obviously interfere with the best land-drainage, solid building, correct measuring, and judicious [drilling]. . . . In fact, he had a reverential soul with a strong practical intelligence. . . . [H]e was one of those precious men within his own district whom everybody would choose to work for them, because he did his work well, charged very little, and often declined to charge at all.

Eliot loves all her characters but doesn't respect them all equally. There's none in the vast gallery of *Middlemarch* that she respects more than Caleb Garth.

It would be a hard world, and a hard-hearted novel, if everyone received exactly what he or she deserved. Fred Vincy, Rosamond's brother, is also spoiled and selfish, though less conniving. He has wasted his university education, borrowed money (from Garth) that he is unable to pay back, and coasted along on (unfounded, as it turns out) expectations of an inheritance. He is rescued from a life of failure by the love of his childhood sweetheart, Mary Garth, the plain but merry and sensible daughter of Caleb. Unlike the typical modern heroine, Mary repeatedly tells Fred that she cannot love him unconditionally, but only if he will take up some proper work like a self-respecting man – like her father, in fact, for whom Fred eventually winds up working happily and productively.

For the most part, though, in *Middlemarch* as in life, character is destiny. Perhaps a more accurate formula would be: character refined by suffering is destiny. Fred's thoughtlessness must be tempered by the very real prospect of losing Mary. Dorothea's disregard of the traditional

J. M.W. Turner's *Coventry, Warwickshire*, c. 1832.

meanings of marriage, making of it instead a pure, disembodied discipleship, teaches her a grudging respect for common sense and a necessary measure of distrust for her enthusiasms.

In *Middlemarch* as in life, character is destiny. Perhaps a more accurate formula would be: character refined by suffering is destiny.

If there is a master insight in *Middlemarch*, a touchstone of the novel's moral wisdom, it is this:

> If we had a keen vision and feeling of all ordinary human life, it would be like hearing the grass grow and the squirrel's heart beat, and we should die of that roar which lies on the other side of silence. As it is, the quickest of us walk about well wadded with stupidity.

The most important thing in this famous passage is not the tremendous metaphor – "the roar which lies on the other side of silence" – but the word "stupidity." In Eliot's moral philosophy, our original sin is not malice or any other positive evil but our deafness and short-sightedness about the needs and feelings of others. Unwadding our ears – a gradual process, if we are not to be overwhelmed by that roar – can only be the result of chastening experience. Our own pain teaches us to notice the pain of others.

At the novel's close, Casaubon has died, and Dorothea has married Ladislaw. They live in London, where he is taking a small but energetic part in the ferment of English political reform in the 1830s. Tenderly appraising Dorothea's once-shining hopes, Eliot draws a moral that fits everyone in the novel – and out of it:

> Her full nature . . . spent itself in channels which had no great name on the earth. But the effect of her being on those around her was incalculably diffusive: for the growing good of the world is partly dependent on unhistoric acts; and that things are not so ill with you and me as they might have been, is half owing to the number who lived faithfully a hidden life, and rest in unvisited tombs.

"To live faithfully a hidden life" is a beautiful ideal, a conception of holiness, sacred or secular, that is all the finer because it is accessible to every human soul.

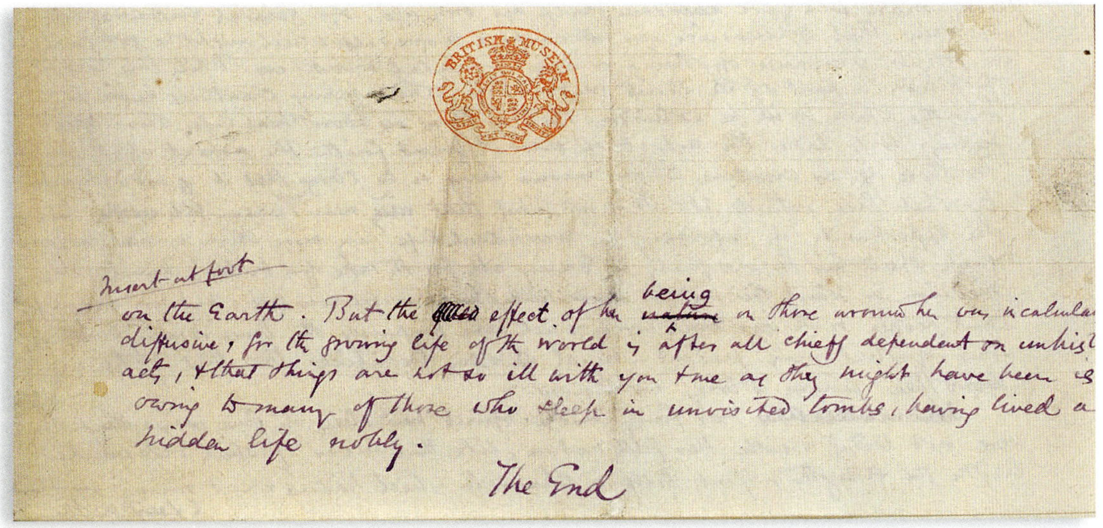
Insert at foot
on the Earth. But the effect of her being on those around her was incalcula
diffusive; for the growing life of the world is after all chiefly dependent on unhist
acts, & that things are not so ill with you & me as they might have been is
owing to many of those who sleep in unvisited tombs, having lived a
hidden life nobly.
The End

Manuscript of Eliot's oft-quoted last paragraph of *Middlemarch*, 1872.

The Fight Against Mammon

EBERHARD ARNOLD

This abridged excerpt from *Salt and Light* (Plough, 2025) is based on a lecture series *Plough*'s founding editor, Eberhard Arnold, gave in Germany from October 1923 to January 1924 under the heading "The God Mammon." His audiences were still coming to terms with Germany's defeat in World War I and the horror and pointlessness of that conflict. The subsequent economic collapse had led to hyperinflation, unemployment, and malnutrition, resulting in a rise in political violence from extremist factions both fascist and socialist, though few could have anticipated the coming atrocities of Nazism and Stalinism. Many were ready to write off a Christianity that had blessed imperial conquest and, with rising inequality spawned by industrialism, sought to appease the poor with the promise of heaven. Knowing all this, Arnold demonstrated how the teachings of Jesus were directly applicable and relevant – as they are today, despite another century of war, capitalist excess, and Christian complicity. *—The Editors*

WHENEVER WE LOOK for a way to consecrate our lives, whenever a longing for devotion arises in us, whenever people seek religion, they are faced with an either-or, with the question of God or mammon.

But it is an error to think that everything religious engenders unity, and that everything irreligious belongs to the other side. To depict the truth of the matter in a deeper sense, one would have to draw a very different dividing line, one that cuts right across the religious and the nonreligious.

Everything that goes by the name of religion is related to a power that carries on its activity independently of us humans. And yet it must still be asked whether all relationships relate to the same center or essential content. With many who call themselves Christians and confess to the name of Jesus Christ, it is questionable whether their religion has anything to do with God, the Father of the Messiah, and his coming kingdom. In fact, one must ask if their religion is not really that of the antigod. Isn't religion, including Christianity, permeated by demonic powers of the abyss that have brought about the disintegration of all human solidarity? Is the great world organization that names itself after Christ not serving a god other than the God and Father whom Jesus confessed, the God of a totally different order? Hasn't the world church, which in practice has sided with wealth and protected it, sanctified mammon, christened warships, and blessed soldiers going into war, in essence denied him whom it confesses with words? And isn't the Christian state the most anti-divine institution that ever existed? Isn't it clear that a government that protects privilege and wealth as well as the organized church is diametrically opposed to the future that God will bring about when Jesus establishes his order of justice? . . .

It is relatively unknown that early Christianity recognized in all sharpness that the religiosity of the present world epoch is actually hostile to

God. The message brought into the world by the first witnesses of the Christ was the message of a completely different kingdom, built on the transvaluation of all values.[1] The first Christians bore witness to this message of the totally new order to come, calling it the message wrapped in mystery, concealed from those who are lost, since their minds have been clouded, and their eyes blinded, by the god of this world (2 Cor. 4:4).

In opposition to the God of the beginning and the end – the God of the future who will establish the coming kingdom of Jesus Christ, with its justice, unity, and love – stands the interim god, the god of this age. This god is the spirit of this world, the earth spirit, brought close to us today in modern literature.[2] This god of greed, of murderous possessiveness, of grasping and holding, is the spirit of this world. By contrast, the first witnesses of Jesus testify that in receiving him, we have not received the spirit of this world, but the Spirit that searches the depths of God, the Spirit that none can know unless they are known by him (1 Cor. 2:10–12).

NOBODY CAN SERVE TWO MASTERS; therefore no one can serve both God and mammon (Matt. 6:24). Jesus defined with utmost sharpness the nature of this mammon spirit. He unmasked the religiousness of the propertied classes and showed how those who live in this sphere worship a spirit of death and murder. It is through this spirit that wars break out; through this spirit lust becomes a tool of commerce. . . .

Even a blind person can see that we have reached a historic juncture where the flowering of the mammon spirit spells incessant death – the death of hundreds and thousands of people. It is because of the deceitful powers inherent in this spirit that it is possible for big business to predominate as it does. Just as we experienced during the war that lying belongs to murder, as its twin, and just as it is impossible to wage a war without a basic level of mendacity – in the same way, a capitalistic society can be maintained only by lying, by duping the public. . . .

If we really turned our attention to the problem, if we saw how common and widespread injustice is – without the world's conscience being aroused by it, let alone rising up against it – we would instantly realize the real situation. In a single flash of recognition, we would see that capitalism by its very nature involves injustice, and that recognition would be enough to set off an uprising against the greatest deception of humankind in world history. . . .

Mammon is money ruling over people. Subjected to the dominion of money ourselves, we lack the strength to rebel against its rule. Whenever life is dependent on income and finances, that is mammon. And because we are dependent in precisely this way – because our personal lives are broken by our enslavement to mammon – we are not in a position to apply the lever that lifts the locked door off its hinges. And yet we are able to recognize that money is the real enemy of God.

God or mammon. Money or spirit. This is the question. As spirit, God is the foundation of our deepest relationships, the innermost fellowship of everything that is alive. All people have an ongoing mutual relationship with other people; no one lives in true isolation. All are interrelated somehow – in groups, families, classes, professions; in nations, states, churches, and all kinds of associations. But these are not their only connections; simply by virtue of being human, they are also interrelated in a much deeper way, as members of the great, growing communion of humankind.

God can grant us the richest relationships imaginable, relationships of love between person and person, spirit and spirit, heart and heart – relationships that lead to organic, constructive fellowship. But there is a devilish

1. The phrase "transvaluation of all values" is from Friedrich Nietzsche, *The Antichrist*.
2. The silent film *Erdgeist* (Earth Spirit), based on Frank Wedekind's play of the same title, was released in the same year Arnold was writing.

Previous spread: Erin Hanson, *Olympic Sunset*, oil on canvas, 2025.

means of robbing even the most spiritual relationship of God, and switching off the flow of love, as it were, from heart to heart. That means is money.

Money is the objectification of all human relationships. Money redirects relationships until finally the only value left is money. Property and money are the means used by the satanic power to destroy our highest goals in life. This fact makes itself felt more and more as money becomes a commodity in itself instead of a means of barter; in the end, all we have left is money itself: money as power. Money acquires significance because so many people are connected with each other solely through it, with no trace of any deeper relationships. Money basically excludes all true fellowship. Banking takes its place.

Money and love are mutually exclusive; money is the opposite of love, just as the sexual defilement of bodies is the opposite of love; just as killing in war is the radical opposite of giving life; just as lying is the opposite of telling the truth.

When mammon rules, it rules soul and spirit. It would be impossible for big business to have such power to enslave and murder, except for the dominion exerted by the mammon spirit. Under this dominion the possessive will is stronger than the will to community; the struggle for survival expressed in mutual readiness to kill is stronger than the urge to love, stronger than the spirit of mutual help; destructive powers are stronger than constructive ones; matter is stronger than spirit; things and circumstances count for more than God; self-assertion is stronger than the spirit of solidarity that brings about fellowship. Instead of setting people in motion and inspiring them to work in a creative way for the life of fellowship, the mammon spirit has engendered an enslavement and scorn of the soul that has made us more subject to circumstance than religious people have ever been subject to God. Because of this reality, everything concerning the god of mammon becomes a thoroughly religious question. In truth, this spirit – the spirit of lying, impurity, and murder – is the spirit of weakness and death.

JESUS DECLARED WAR on this spirit. He conquered it by overwhelming it; by healing victims of sickness and decay with his power. Jesus, the prince of life, declared himself the enemy of death. He lived among us to take away death's power and to destroy it, as the devil's work (1 John 3:8). Here death is overcome by the Spirit of life that proceeds from Christ and brings about the fellowship of all living things. Christ was so conscious of this that he exclaimed, "Now is the judgment of this world; now the prince of this world will be cast out" (John 12:31). And the Holy Spirit convinces us that this prince has been defeated (John 16:11).

We are now compelled to ask how Jesus conducted this fight. Did he not say, "Make friends for yourselves through unjust mammon" (Luke 16:9)? Did he not say, "Give back to Caesar what is Caesar's" (Matt. 22:21)? How can we reconcile these commands with these other words of his: "Do not lay up treasures for yourselves on earth" (Matt. 6:19), "Woe to you who are rich; woe to you who are full" (Luke 6:24–25); and, "If someone sues you for your coat, give him your cloak as well" (Matt. 5:40)?

To examine each separate saying would lead us too far afield. It must suffice to recognize the sum total of Jesus' stand. As soon as we side with him, we will be ready to give up mammon, to declare war on it, and to overcome its power in our lives. When our inmost eye has opened to the vision of Christ's light, our eyes will stop yielding to mammon's beck and call (Matt. 6:22–23). Once our hearts are set on the new future and on the hope that God will establish a new kingdom, we will no longer want to amass property. We

---

Eberhard Arnold (1883–1935), a German theologian, was cofounder of the Bruderhof and the founding editor of Plough.

will strive only for this one thing and turn our backs on everything else. We will live for the future – for the freedom and unity and peace of all humankind. Then the saying, "Make friends for yourselves through unjust mammon," will be truly fulfilled – because in giving away our money, we will gain the love of friends who will have fellowship with us forever.

When that pure-minded rich youth, who was not aware of having done anything wrong, came to Jesus, Jesus loved him at first sight and asked him whether he loved God and his neighbor. The youth thought he had done as he ought in every way. "Good," said Jesus, "If this is really so, then what you must do now is to make this love real. Go and sell everything you have, give it to the poor, and come with me" (Matt. 19:16–21).

When Jesus entered the temple, the god he encountered was not his God, but mammon – the god of cattle and cattle dealers, banks and bankers. And Jesus made a whip, not to strike people, but to forcibly overturn the tables and show his contempt for money by dashing it to the floor. He testified that the temple should not belong to mammon but to God (Matt. 21:12–13). And when a trickster showed him a piece of money, the coin of the emperor, the head of the state, and asked him what to do with it, he answered that we should give to Satan what belongs to Satan: "Give to Caesar what belongs to Caesar, and to God what belongs to God."

When the itinerant disciples needed someone to keep and manage their common purse, it was Judas who was chosen – Judas, whom Jesus knew would become his betrayer (John 12:6). The murderer from the beginning was thus exposed in the very company of Jesus' disciples (John 8:44). And he met his end as every murderer must. He disclosed the secret of Jesus' messiahship by revealing him who, when asked by the political and religious authorities, "Are you the Messiah, the son of the Highest?" stood his ground and answered, "I am; you shall see the Son of Man seated at the right hand of Power, and coming on the clouds of heaven" (Mark 14:61–62). Jesus was put to death on the basis of this revolutionary confession.

After this dramatic attack on the mammonistic order, the Spirit-born community was seemingly destroyed, since its leader had been killed and eliminated.

Erin Hanson, *Gnarled Storm*, oil on canvas, 2011.

Among religious and irreligious people alike, the power of money seemed to triumph; the will of mammon and of death seemed to have gained the upper hand.

Yet through the very execution of the leader of this new order, through the grave itself, life won out. From the downtrodden people of Judea, young men and women gathered and waited together for something new – for the spirit of love, order, and freedom that they knew to be the Spirit of God's kingdom. And the Spirit came upon them and formed a church, a fellowship of work and goods, in which everything belonged to all, and all were active to the full extent of their varied powers and gifts (Acts 2: 43–47).

And yet even this fellowship succumbed to the deadly process that destroys life. Just as individuals die, so this church also died. But over the course of centuries, new church communities arose. Time and again, small communities were formed in which men and women together declared war on mammon and together took upon themselves the poverty of generosity. In actual fact, by choosing such poverty, they went the way of true wealth. People filled with this urge of love can be found through the centuries. We hear their voices, we join hands with them across the passage of time. We feel a kinship of faith with them – faith for the future. . . .

We can have no part in violent revolution. Whichever side sheds blood is on the side of the father of lies. People are deceiving themselves if they think they can overcome mammon by arming themselves, relying on the same spirit of the abyss as mammon itself. The new can only be born of the new. You cannot use poison to get rid of poison. Life can only be born of life. Love can only be born of love. Community can arise only out of the will for community.

Our way to the goal is the communal way of brotherliness, where, as we walk, we will meet other small bands of people, ready to be merged in the one goal, to belong to the one future.

Already now we can live in the power of this future. Already now we can shape our lives in the presence of the coming God, and in accordance with his kingdom. The victory of the Spirit is already manifest through the church community. The kingdom of love, free of mammon, is approaching this earth; it is very close. And so we must change our thinking radically – we must change radically, so that we are ready for the order of things to come.

> Come now, you rich people, weep and wail for the miseries that are coming to you. Your riches have rotted, and your clothes are moth-eaten. Your gold and silver have rusted, and their rust will be evidence against you, and it will eat your flesh like fire. You have laid up treasure during the last days. Listen! The wages of the laborers who mowed your fields, which you kept back by fraud, cry out, and the cries of the harvesters have reached the ears of the Lord of hosts. You have lived on the earth in luxury and in pleasure; you have nourished your hearts in a day of slaughter. You have condemned and murdered the righteous one, who does not resist you.
>
> Be patient, therefore, brothers and sisters, until the coming of the Lord (James 5:1–7).

Singing in Community

At the Bruderhof, music is worship, fellowship, and fun.

MAUREEN SWINGER

In conversations with friends who visit Bruderhof communities, the subject of music surfaces frequently – primarily because music itself surfaces frequently here.

In fact, singing has always been an intrinsic part of Bruderhof culture. Today our church is an international network of communities, but it began as a handful of seekers who left private life and moved together to form one household in 1920, in Germany. Our continued musical emphasis has roots in the cultural heritage of those first members. Many came to the community directly from the German Youth Movement, a free-spirited constellation of young people whose interest in "purer" pre-industrial traditions led to the rediscovery of medieval carols and folk songs, and the subsequent compilation of songbooks that became popular across the country.

The German Youth Movement wasn't organized or cohesive, but was comprised of many small groups of young people who fled urban living with the stated goal of escaping the rigidity of their conventional society. These *Wandervögel* ("birds of passage") enjoyed taking guitars and violins up to the top of a hill, building a fire, passing around some bread and cheese, then singing ballads and arguing passionately about philosophy and the truths to be found in music and in the beauty of the natural world. In direct reaction to the stuffy Lutheran piety of the day, many were not prepared to confine truth and beauty to the God preached in the pews. But perhaps unawares, they were encountering the living God as they actively searched for the spirit behind these good things.

As some of these seekers made their way to a Bruderhof community, there was clearly a strong

A fireside sing-along at the Plough Writers Weekend, Fox Hill Bruderhof, 2023.

spiritual current at work – a longing to bring the ideal of brotherhood to expression not only in the practical aspects of daily life, but in music, song, and dance as well, whether at mealtimes, evening gatherings, or seasonal celebrations.

The continuity of that vision is represented in the songs we sing today – for example, our current Christmas hymnal, comprising over three hundred songs, has its origins in these earliest years of our community. Some of the songs are taken from the Bruderhof's very first collection, *Sonnenlieder* ("Songs of the Sun"), a 1924 publication. Others were collected from a hand-lettered anthology compiled in 1934.

Singing – whether in family circles, children's groups, worship meetings, or plays and concerts – has remained an important part of Bruderhof life, especially during Lent and Advent. And as war and political upheaval forced the community to move from country to country, new songs were added to the canon. In England, one of the Bruderhof's first places of refuge from Nazi Germany, new members brought with them the *Oxford Book of Carols*, first published in 1928. In the 1950s – the decade the Bruderhof put down its first roots in New York – involvement in the American work camp movement, with its emphasis on international understanding and cooperation, led to the rediscovery of folk tunes from around the globe. Traditional American hymns joined English translations of the Lutheran ones the first generation loved. Later chapters of our communal history brought us the addition of African-American spirituals, melodies from the hollows of Appalachia, and songs learned from South Korea, Zimbabwe, and South Africa.

Of course, during the holidays, there's always a flurry of rehearsals and performances of plays and pageants, and numerous songs from these productions have found their way into our yearly celebrations, as have choruses from Vivaldi's *Gloria*, Handel's *Messiah*, and the oratorios by Bach and Saint-Saëns, not to mention the ageless hymns and carols still sung by millions around the world.

AS A CHILD, I always decided in Advent that Christmas was my favorite time of year, only to have Easter supplant it every spring. The songs usher a child through Palm Sunday and all of Holy Week, communicating the sacrifice and sorrow of Good Friday as no sermon ever could. But they also welcome the sunrise of Easter morning with the triumph of trumpets. "Christ the Lord Is Risen Today" and "Crown Him with Many Crowns" ring out, intermingled with no less lovely songs composed by Bruderhof members over the years – perhaps an inspired kindergarten teacher might come up with a few simple verses to welcome spring and Eastertide with her students:

All the earth is waking from her winter sleep;
Snow and ice are going, streams and rivers flowing,
Easter now has come again.

Gone are cold and sorrow,
Jesus we will follow,
Let us all together praise our risen Lord.

When kids grow up hearing and then singing these songs, favorite songs become synonymous with their page number. Last Easter morning, when our community gathered to sing the victorious songs of resurrection, I couldn't help smiling when several children's voices piped up, "One sixty-three!" at the same time – my own childhood favorite, a poem by Jane Tyson Clement set to music by my husband's grandmother, composer Marlys Swinger:

The lambs leap in the meadow,
the larks leap in the sky,
And all the bells of heaven ring
because our Lord rides by.

Maureen Swinger is an editor at Plough *and lives at the Fox Hill Bruderhof in Walden, New York, with her husband, Jason, and their three children.*

MANY OF THE SONGS we sing, though, have no great spiritual heft. Communal lunches frequently begin with a cheery song about whatever season we find ourselves in – and whatever the kids might be doing while out in it – sledding, skating, hiking, camping, jumping in leaf piles.

But, in keeping with the *Sonnenlieder* book of old, it still is the most astonishing mash-up. In the well-worn pages of the *Sing Joyfully* songbook, affectionately known as "The Blue Book" (because there are also red, green, and even purple anthologies), we have seasonal songs that boast lyrics by William Shakespeare, William Blake, and Thomas Nashe. One of the Blake poems is set to a Russian folk tune. Then there's a melody borrowed from Mozart, with some lyrics by Aldis Dunbar, and some by a Bruderhof member who doubtless added in another verse because "the song was too short."

Summer's in the hills today,
Laughter in the breeze – O listen!
Summer's in the woods today,
Fluttering the aspen trees.

There are songs to acknowledge the arrival of a new baby:

We thank you, loving God
For every little thing,
But for babies, sweet and small
We thank you most of all.

Also, about twenty different birthday songs to mix it up from the ubiquitous "Happy Birthday to You" chant. Who wouldn't want to receive such a blessing as this one on their next year of life?

We wish you the glow of the sun by day,
The shine of the stars by night,
On your path, the gleam of the moon's soft ray,
And the fireflies' twinkling light.

It's as if music is its own language, drawn on to announce the seasons, rejoice in whatever needs celebrating (a *lot* needs celebrating), underscore faith, bear grief together. This undercurrent of music goes beyond the subject matter of the songs themselves. Any given sing-along takes on its own character, often with a surprising, apparently random combination of songs brought into the flow.

Even the songs sung at worship meetings might not always overtly refer to God. In a hark-back to some of the anti-formal-religious sentiments of the 1920s German Youth Movement, many from the great wave of young American families and singles who joined the Bruderhof in the fifties and sixties had stepped away from a denominational church, searching for something to believe in, yet reluctant to use religious language lightly. They brought with them a wealth of songs picked up from summer camps and conferences, or passed along from friends or family.

Thus, at the close of an evening worship meeting, you might hear someone suggest a song that came our way years ago via – of all sources – the Girl Scouts:

Peace I ask of thee, O River,
Peace, peace, peace.
When I learn to live serenely,
Cares will cease.
From the hills I gather courage,
Vision of the day to be,
Strength to lead and faith to follow,
All are given unto me.

While the author probably intended the peace and faith and vision to be generic enough for many beliefs or none – "spiritual but not religious" – here, in a gathering of scripture reading and prayer, the hills that give us courage could be the same ones we lifted our eyes to for help. The river might as well be the one whose streams make glad the city of God.

IN A TIME when the word "music" mostly brings to mind digitized, commercialized, and performative sound – the act of "singing to" – it is still possible to reclaim the earlier, richer understanding of music, "singing with." Communal singing is so different from performance: the latter delivers an experience to an audience, who encounter the music as receivers, while the former invites participation. It is a circle, balanced, equalizing, full but never finished, sending out sound to beckon outliers to lend their voices for the joy and comfort of it.

This is why it doesn't really matter to me if we're singing worship songs or folk songs, or really any other genre. As long as we're a group of people with common purpose, we are giving thanks for being together, which means we're also thanking the One who brings us together.

YOU MIGHT LIKE TO THINK that cradle immersion in a culture of music would secure the blessings of perfect pitch on ourselves and our posterity. Alas, it does not. It's true that between the general surround-sound and the various inspired music teachers who strum guitars and introduce age-appropriate songs to the one-year-olds, many kids can warble the treble line of a few hundred songs by the time they reach middle school, and some can figure out harmonizing just by hearing enough of it. But it's not given to everyone to make like a bird, and that's fine. One of my favorite uncles, Tony Potts, would happily rumble along in a somewhat tuneless baritone, just obeying the general command of Psalm 100 to "make a joyful noise unto the Lord." Others who have gifts in nonmusical directions may opt to just listen and appreciate, while still contributing by being part of the circle.

And if someone is suffering or grieving, sometimes there is comfort in being silent within the sound, like a rock that feels the strength of water flowing over and around it.

GROWING UP on a veritable river of music was not something I was aware of as an appreciable thing until my husband, Jason, and I spent a few years living in a smaller house community. Yes, we were surrounded by as much performative music as we chose to spool up. Yes, we sang a lot together, because the kids were little and we wanted to keep our favorite songs alive, a communicative link to our culture as well as our faith.

A mini-band was OK; we sang to wake ourselves up at breakfast, and drift the children to sleep at night. The sound felt a little thin and lonely around Easter and Christmas. I was more than delighted when friends in our kids' play group expressed interest in learning some of our repertoire of spring songs for a neighborhood May Day celebration, then happily adopted the Bruderhof's "lantern walk" tradition in fall, with all its enchanting accompanying songs.

But I was totally unprepared for my response to the daily Bruderhof singing upon our family's arrival at Fox Hill community a few years later. All those bookless, audience-less, effortless, two-hundred-voice four-part harmonies poured over me; it was like standing under a waterfall.

It did not matter in the least what song was being sung. It was all prayer.

Friends from Honesdale, Pennsylvania, join Fox Hill community members to share favorite folk songs and hymns.

SUSANNAH BLACK ROBERTS

A Gadfly of God

Justin Martyr, like Socrates before him, was convicted of being an atheist.

JUSTIN HIMSELF TELLS THE STORY this way. It was the thirteenth year of the reign of Emperor Hadrian, 883 *ab urbe condita*. We would call it AD 130. Justin was in his early twenties, going for a walk near the sea – the Aegean, as he was in Ephesus, in Asia Minor. This was not just a saunter: he was a serious young man doing what serious young men love to do, which is to have a Big Philosophical Think.

Justin had a lot of material to work with. He'd been born in Flavia Neapolis, in Palestinian Syria, a pagan citizen of the Roman Empire. Beginning in his teens, he had felt himself to be on a philosophical quest: What is the nature of reality, of justice? What leads to happiness? And what about God? Or is it "the gods"?

He'd burned through quite a few teachers in the time he'd been on this project. He'd started with a Stoic, who was no help: "He did not himself know anything about God, and said such instruction was unnecessary." Then he went to a Peripatetic, who entertained him for a couple of days but then tried to charge him a fee, which Justin felt to be a red flag. After that, he'd tried a Pythagorean, but

Ruins at the ancient city of Ephesus.

the Pythagorean said he couldn't possibly begin teaching Justin philosophy until he had learned music, astronomy, and geometry, and kicked him out when he admitted that he didn't want to wait to start studying philosophy until he'd gotten through math.

Justin seemed to fare better with the Platonists. "The perception of immaterial things quite overpowered me, and the contemplation of ideas furnished my mind with wings, so that in a little while I supposed that I had become wise, and such was my stupidity, I expected immediately to look upon God, for this is the end of Plato's philosophy." It was in this state that he came to the seaside.

And as he walked, he realized he was being watched; his watcher was an old man, with the air of one who also is seeking. The dialogue that follows indeed betrays a writer who had been reading a lot of Plato.

> Old Man: Do you know me?
>
> Justin: No.
>
> Old Man: Why, then, do you so look at me?
>
> Justin: I am astonished, because you have chanced to be in my company in the same place; for I had not expected to see any man here.
>
> Old Man: I am concerned about some of my household. These have gone away from me; and therefore I have come to make personal search for them, if, perhaps, they shall make their appearance somewhere. But why are you here?

Justin explains that he is a philosopher:

> Justin: What greater work could one accomplish than this, to show the reason which governs all, and having laid hold of it, and being mounted upon it, to look down on the errors of others, and their pursuits? But without philosophy and right reason, prudence would not be present to any man. Wherefore it is necessary for every man to philosophize, and to esteem this the greatest and most honorable work . . .
>
> Old Man (interrupting): Does philosophy, then, make happiness?
>
> Justin: Assuredly, and it alone.
>
> Old Man: What, then, is philosophy? And what is happiness? Pray tell me, unless something hinders you from saying.
>
> Justin: Philosophy, then, is the knowledge of that which really exists, and a clear perception of the truth; and happiness is the reward of such knowledge and wisdom.
>
> Old Man: But what do you call God?
>
> Justin: That which always maintains the same nature, and in the same manner, and is the cause of all other things – that, indeed, is God.

The old man, he tells us, listened to him "with pleasure," though even now we get the sense that this young man is perhaps a bit full of himself. But this is how Socrates worked: to draw these confident young men into making statements, and then to examine these statements from every side, to pass from apparent knowledge into ignorance and then, perhaps, gradually, to something else that is more solid.

Indeed, after this initial exchange, Justin naturally falls into the role of one of Socrates' interlocutors, giving himself all the "It is as you say" lines. The Old Man prods at Justin's certainties, without entirely disagreeing with the natural theology he has come to espouse, and winds up thus:

> There existed, long before this time, certain men more ancient than all those who are esteemed philosophers, both righteous and beloved by God,

---

Susannah Black Roberts is a senior editor of Plough. *She and her husband, Alastair Roberts, split their time between New York City and the United Kingdom.*

> who spoke by the Divine Spirit. . . . They are called prophets. These alone both saw and announced the truth to men . . . speaking those things alone which they saw and which they heard. . . . Their writings are still extant, and he who has read them is very much helped in his knowledge of . . . those matters which the philosopher ought to know. . . .
>
> They were witnesses to the truth above all demonstration, and worthy of belief; and those events which have happened . . . compel you to assent to the utterances made by them, although, indeed, they were entitled to credit on account of the miracles which they performed, since they both glorified the Creator, the God and Father of all things, and proclaimed his Son, the Christ [sent] by him. . . . But pray that, above all things, the gates of light may be opened to you; for these things cannot be perceived or understood by all, but only by the one to whom God and his Christ have imparted wisdom.

They talk on and on through the day, and then the old man goes away, leaving Justin to reflect on the encounter: "I have not seen him since. But straightway a flame was kindled in my soul; and a love of the prophets, and of those men who are friends of Christ, possessed me; and while revolving his words in my mind, I found this philosophy alone to be safe and profitable. Thus, and for this reason, I am a philosopher."

He is telling this story many years later, at his first meeting with a man who would become a friend. He is still in Ephesus: they meet under the shaded promenade around the city's gymnasium. Trypho, a Hellenized Jew, also a Roman citizen, had started out the conversation by calling out to him, "Hail, O philosopher!" – as Justin was dressed in the *pallium*, the cloak sported by philosophers.

Throughout their dialogue, Justin speaks as a philosopher to another lover of wisdom. He speaks as a Gentile follower of the God of Israel. And he speaks as a Christian. Elsewhere (in the two Apologies, which, along with the *Dialogue with Trypho*, are the only works of his that remain to us) he speaks as a former pagan, to others who were raised as he was on the stories of Perseus and Aesclepius, Zeus and Hera – or Jupiter and Juno – and all their crowd. He is all things to all people. His approach is profoundly helpful in our own age, full of contradictory takes on the apprehension of reality, the conduct of one's life, the pursuit of happiness, and the knowledge of God.

Justin is bold in what he claims, bolder than most Christians today would be:

> We have been taught that Christ is the first-born of God, and we have declared above that he is the Word of whom every race of men were partakers; and those who lived reasonably are Christians, even though they have been thought atheists; as, among the Greeks, Socrates and Heraclitus, and men like them. . . .
>
> When Socrates endeavored, by true reason and examination, to bring these things to light, and deliver men from the demons, then the demons themselves, by means of men who rejoiced in iniquity, compassed his death, as an atheist and a profane person, on the charge that he was introducing new divinities; and in our case they display a similar activity.
>
> For not only among the Greeks did reason [*Logos*] prevail to condemn these things through Socrates, but also among the Barbarians were they condemned by Reason Himself, who took shape, and became man, and was called Jesus Christ; and in obedience to him, we not only deny that they who did such things as these are gods, but assert that they are wicked and impious demons. . . .
>
> Hence are we called atheists. And we confess that we are atheists, so far as gods of this sort are concerned, but not with respect to the most true God, the Father of righteousness and temperance and the other virtues, who is free from all impurity. Him, and the Son . . . and the prophetic Spirit, we worship and adore, knowing them in reason and

Photograph by Lynel via AdobeStock. Used by permission.

> truth, and declaring without grudging to everyone who wishes to learn, as we have been taught.

He was killed. It's there in the name: Justin Martyr. He was martyred in Rome under the emperor Marcus Aurelius, philosopher-king if ever there was one, author of elegant books of Stoic epigrams. His judge was the prefect Quintus Junius Rusticus, himself a philosopher and Marcus Aurelius's teacher.

These men did not themselves believe in the gods. But it was for refusing to worship those gods that Justin was tried and convicted. He was accused of being an atheist, impious, not paying respect to the gods whom the state respects, of being an introducer of new and strange gods. We have a reliable eyewitness account of the trial:

> The saints were seized and brought before the prefect of Rome, whose name was Rusticus. As they stood before the judgement seat, Rusticus said to Justin: "Above all, have faith in the gods and obey the emperors."
>
> Justin: We cannot be accused or condemned for obeying the commands of our Savior, Jesus Christ.
>
> Rusticus: What system of teaching do you profess?
>
> Justin: I have tried to learn about every system, but I have accepted the true doctrines of the Christians.
>
> Rusticus: What sort of teaching is that?
>
> Justin: Worship the God of the Christians. We hold him to be from the beginning the one creator and maker of the whole creation, of things seen and things unseen. We worship also the Lord Jesus Christ, the Son of God. He was foretold by the prophets as the future herald of salvation for the human race and the teacher of distinguished disciples. For myself, since I am a human being, I consider that what I say is insignificant in comparison with his infinite godhead. I acknowledge the existence of a prophetic power, for the one I have just spoken of as the Son of God was the subject of prophecy. I know that the prophets

Mosaic floor in the ancient city of Ephesus.

were inspired from above when they spoke of his coming among men.

Rusticus would not have imagined himself to be Pilate here. Nor would he have seen himself as Antiochus IV Epiphanes, demanding that the seven Maccabean sons break the Torah. But he certainly could have recalled Meletus throwing the accusation of atheism and impiety at Socrates. One can imagine Socrates' own words at the back of Rusticus's mind:

> If now when the god orders me to fulfill the philosopher's mission . . . I were to desert my post . . . I might justly be arraigned in court for denying the existence of the gods, if I disobeyed the oracle because I was afraid of death: then I should be fancying that I was wise when I was not wise. . . .
>
> If you kill such a one as I am, you will injure yourselves more than you will injure me. . . . And now, Athenians, I am not going to argue for my own sake, as you may think, but for yours, that you may not sin against the god, or lightly reject his boon by condemning me. . . .
>
> So, now, we all go our ways – I to die, and you to live. And the question is, which one of us on either side is going toward something that is better? It is not clear, except to the god.

"Worship the God of the Christians. We hold him to be from the beginning the one creator and maker of the whole creation, of things seen and things unseen."

—Justin Martyr

Socrates worshiped what he did not know. Justin lived in the world of the Proclamation, of what Saint Peter called "the things that have now been announced to you through those who preached the good news to you by the Holy Spirit sent from heaven." These are things "into which angels long to look," things, as Jesus said, quoting the psalmist, "hidden since the foundations of the world."

> The prefect said to Justin: "You are called a learned man. . . . Listen: if you were scourged and beheaded . . . do you have an idea that you will go up to heaven to receive some suitable rewards?"
>
> Justin: It is not an idea that I have; it is something I know well. . . .
>
> Rusticus: Now let us come to the point at issue. . . . Gather round then and with one accord offer sacrifice to the gods.
>
> Justin: No one who is right thinking stoops from true worship to false worship.
>
> . . . Rusticus pronounced sentence, saying: "Let those who have refused to sacrifice to the gods and to obey the command of the emperor be scourged and led away to suffer capital punishment according to the ruling of the laws." Glorifying God, the holy martyrs went out to the accustomed place. They were beheaded, and so fulfilled their witness of martyrdom in confessing their faith in their Savior.

"I dare say," said Socrates, "that you may feel irritated at being suddenly awakened when you are caught napping; and you may think that if you were to strike me dead . . . then you would sleep on for the remainder of your lives, unless the god in his care of you gives you another gadfly."

Here, 563 years later, facing that philosophical jurist, the representative of that most philosophical emperor, was another gadfly.

Theophanes the Cretan, *Saint Justin Martyr*, ca. 1545.